THE
ULTIMATE
PSYCHOMETRIC
TEST BOOK

over 1,000 test questions with explanations

MIKE BRYON

**KOGAN
PAGE**

London & Philadelphia

I dedicate this book to my wife, Lola

Publisher's note
Every possible effort has been made to ensure that the information contained in this book is accurate at the time of going to press, and the publishers and authors cannot accept responsibility for any errors or omissions, however caused. No responsibility for loss or damage occasioned to any person acting, or refraining from action, as a result of the material in this publication can be accepted by the editor, the publisher or any of the authors.

First published in Great Britain and the United States in 2006 by Kogan Page Limited
Reprinted 2006, 2007

120 Pentonville Road
London N1 9JN
United Kingdom
www.kogan-page.co.uk

525 South 4th Street, #241
Philadelphia PA 19147
USA

© Mike Bryon, 2006

ISBN-10   0 7494 4458 4
ISBN-13   978 0 7494 4458 7

British Library Cataloguing-in-Publication Data

A CIP record for this book is available from the British Library.

Library of Congress Cataloging-in-Publication Data

Bryon, Mike.
    The ultimtate psychometric test book : over 1000 test questions with explanations / Mike Bryon.
        p. cm.
    ISBN 0–7494–4458–4
    1. Employment tests.   2. Employee selection.   3. Psychological tests.
I. Title.
HF5549.5.E5b788 2006
650.14--dc22

                                                                                    2005030514

Typeset by Saxon Graphics Ltd, Derby
Printed and bound in Great Britain by Bell & Bain Ltd, Glasgow

Table of Contents

Preface

From now on, treat a psychometric test as the route to the career of your dreams. Use this book to ensure that you stand head and shoulders above the crowd of other applicants.

We face psychometric tests at so many points in our career and their use is on the increase. At some stage in the selection process for many jobs or courses you will have to take one. For the unprepared candidate they represent a significant challenge; fail and you risk not gaining the job or training of your choice. Take them seriously, as many more people are failed than pass.

Let me help you become one of the candidates that really stand out from the crowd. The secret is practice and mindset. The right sort, the right amount, at the right time and you will succeed.

This is the 'ultimate' psychometric test book because it contains 1,000 realistic practice questions. It is expressly designed for self-study, covers the major types of test and provides essential advice on the winning mindset. It also signposts the reader to the best sources of further practice in the Kogan Page Testing Series.

It is the ideal starting point for the reader who wants to do really well in a psychometric test at the intermediate level and it is the perfect introduction for candidates of graduate-level tests.

You will not find another book with so many practice questions. This means that you can really get down to some serious score-improving preparation. I will describe how to best organize your study and provide many hundreds of explanations and explanatory notes to help make sure you realize where you might be going wrong.

Success in a psychometric test is hard work and I will ask you to make a significant commitment in terms of time and effort. The choice is entirely yours – rise to the challenge and your dream career could become a reality. The alternative is to risk failure.

If you face a test that contains questions of a type not covered by this title or the suggested further reading, then contact me care of Kogan Page and if I know of one I will be glad to let you know of a source of suitable practice material.

May I apologize in advance if you find an error in this book; please do not let it undermine your belief in the value of practice and do please take the trouble to notify me, care of Kogan Page, so that it can be removed at the next reprint.

Psychometric Tests: What Are They?

A psychometric test is not like a blood sample test where you simply roll up your sleeve and feel the discomfort of the needle. You have no control over the outcome of a blood test but in a psychometric test you should be totally in control. You achieve this through hard work, systematic preparation and a good test technique.

Psychometric tests are most often taken with paper and pen or at a computer screen, but they may also be taken when performing a task in a workplace situation or even in a gym or on a running machine.

Whatever the particular task, they will be designed so that a score can be awarded, perhaps it is how long the candidate took or how many questions were completed correctly. The test will allow the test administrator to draw comparisons between candidates and the whole point when used for recruitment is that it will allow the administrator to conclude that candidate A got a better score than candidate B and that candidates F, G, H, I, J and K failed!

If you face a psychometric test as a part of a recruitment process for a job or course of study then it is reasonable to assume that lots of people have applied and there are fewer vacancies or places than applicants. Some organizations attract as many as 40 applicants for every vacancy. The employer or college relies on the test to identify the more suitable candidates in as fair and objective a way as is economically possible. Every applicant will be invited to take the test and the results will be compared to decide who should be invited to the next stage of the recruitment process. The remaining candidates will be rejected.

There are many types of test in use. Some are specific to a particular role or profession, others are general. It may involve a questionnaire completed online or a series of sub-tests taken one after the other over a number of hours at a test centre with only a short pause between the papers. They may be designed to test your stamina and endurance as well as your interests, personality and abilities. Examples include:

- IQ tests;
- verbal reasoning;
- numerical analysis;
- mechanical and technical reasoning;
- diagrammatic and abstract analysis;
- work sample tests;
- in-tray exercises;
- trainability tests;
- personality questionnaires;
- interest and motivational inventories.

These are very broad headings and each would include many different styles and types of question. A questionnaire will not normally have a time limit while a test will be strictly timed.

As soon as you realize that you need to pass a test or complete a questionnaire, go about finding out as much as you can about it. The internet is a great source of this kind of information but the organization that has invited you should provide you with, or direct you to, a description of the test and some sample questions. You will not be able to get hold of past papers or real copies of the test.

If you suffer a disability that will adversely affect your ability to complete the test or any aspect of the recruitment process then inform the organization at the first opportunity. They should be prepared to organize things differently to better accommodate your needs and for certain conditions they may allow extra time to complete the test.

After the test the organization should be willing to provide information on your performance, although you may have to ask for it. They should indicate the areas in which you performed strongly and areas in which you might work to improve. Most will be willing to discuss your score with you over the telephone and this is often the way to get the most valuable feedback.

What to expect on the day

You may have to complete a questionnaire online or at home, returning it with your application form, but you will most likely be invited to attend a training or recruitment centre to take a psychometric test.

Don't be late! And dress smartly. You are likely to be one of many candidates attending that day. If you are to undertake a physical test as well as written papers then you may need to bring along sports clothes and shoes; you may be expected to attend for most of the day. All this detail will be included in your letter of invitation, so read it carefully.

Turn up prepared to work very hard indeed. Doing well in any test is not simply a matter of intelligence or ability. Hard work and determination play a big part too. If at the end of the day you do not feel completely exhausted then you may have not done yourself justice. So go for it.

Expect to attend on the day able to adopt the right mental approach. The candidates that do best are not usually the ones who are fearful or who feel resentment about having to take a test. The winning approach is one in which you attend looking forward to the challenge and the opportunity it represents. You are there to demonstrate your abilities and prove to the organization that you are a suitable candidate. The best candidates approach the test with confidence in themselves and their abilities. This should not discourage you. Everyone can develop this approach. The secret is preparation. Attend the test fully prepared for the challenge and use it to demonstrate how good you have become.

Turn up fully prepared having spent many hours practising for the test, ready to take full advantage of your strengths and having addressed any areas of weakness. Do not underestimate how long it can take to prepare for a test. Start as soon as you receive notice that you must attend.

It is really important that you listen carefully to the instructions provided before a test begins. You may well be feeling nervous and this may affect your concentration so make yourself focus on what is being said. Much of the information will be a repeat of the test description sent to you with the letter inviting you to the test. So read and reread this document before the day of the test.

Pay particular attention to instructions on how many questions there are in each sub-test and be sure you are familiar with the demands of each style of question. Look to see if at the bottom of the page it says 'turn over'. You will be surprised how many people reach the bottom of a page and wrongly conclude that they have reached the end of the questions. They stop working and wait when they should be working away at the remaining questions.

Keep track of the time during the test and manage how long you spend on any one question. You must keep going right up to the end. Aim to get right the balance between speed and accuracy. It is better that you risk getting some questions wrong but attempt every question rather than double-check each answer and be told to stop because you have run out of time before you have finished. Practice can really help develop this skill.

If you hit a difficult section of questions don't lose heart. Keep going – everyone gets some questions wrong. You may find that you come next to a section of questions in which you can excel.

If you do not know the answer to a question then educated guessing is well worth a try. If you are unsure of an answer to a multiple choice question then look at the suggested answers and try ruling some out as wrong. This way you can reduce the number of suggested answers from which to guess and hopefully increase your chances of guessing correctly.

How to Pass Psychometric Tests and How to Use This Book

Doing well in a test is not simply a matter of intelligence but also requires determination and hard work. If passing is important to you then be prepared both to set aside a significant number of hours in which to practise and to work very hard during the real test.

The value of practice

You must seek to achieve the best possible score in a real psychometric test. Other candidates will be trying to do this so you must too, otherwise you risk coming a very poor second.

The secret is practice. Everyone will improve their test score with practice and for many candidates practice will mean the difference between pass and fail.

Practice works best on material that is as much like the questions in the real test as possible. Select from this book questions that are similar to those in the real test that you face and restrict your practice to these questions. I have included material that will benefit most readers but this may mean that not all the material is appropriate to you in terms of the level of difficulty. So select the most appropriate material in terms of the level of difficulty and if necessary obtain further material from other titles in the Kogan Page Testing Series.

Practise right up until the day before the test. Practice, to be effective, must be challenging, painful even. To be sure that you are continuing to improve, make sure that the practice remains a challenge. If it stops being a pain then there really will be very little gain! But before you start practising, first you must get test wise.

Get test wise

Most psychometric tests comprise a series of smaller tests taken one after the other, with a short pause between the papers. They might include, for example, first a sub-test on verbal reasoning, then a numerical reasoning sub-test and finally a non-verbal reasoning sub-test. But this is only one of many possible combinations. The series of sub-tests is called a battery.

It is really important that you understand exactly what the test you face involves. You will be astonished at how many people attend for a test not knowing what to expect. The first time they learn of the type of questions involved is when the test administrator describes them just before the test begins for real. Don't make this mistake. You need to know the nature of the challenge as soon as possible.

The organization to which you have applied should have sent you, with the letter of invitation, a description of the type of questions and the format of the test. If they have not done this then have a look on their website to see if they describe the test there or telephone them and ask them to describe the test. Be sure to have a pen and paper ready and get details on:

- how many sub-tests the test battery comprises;
- what the title of each sub-test is;
- what sort of question makes up a sub-test (ask them to describe an example of each type of question);
- how many questions each sub-test includes;
- how long you are allowed to complete each sub-test;
- whether it is multiple choice or short answer;
- whether you complete it with pen and paper or at a computer terminal;
- whether or not a calculator is allowed.

Armed with this information you can now find hundreds of practice questions on which to set about a systematic programme of preparation.

How much and what kind of practice

Once you have a very clear idea of the test you face, you need to set about finding hundreds of relevant practice questions. You need hundreds because to get the most from practice you should undertake a minimum of 20 hours. If you are weak in maths or English then you may well have to practise a lot more than this. This book contains 1,000 practice questions and will be an ideal source of practice material for many candidates for the majority of tests. But you are unlikely to find all the practice material you need in one publication. This book will best suit the candidate at the intermediate level and introduces material at the graduate level, so if you face a psychometric test for a graduate, managerial or professional position you should move on from this title to other more advanced material also available in the Kogan Page Testing Series. In that series you will find more advanced material as well as publications that offer fuller explanations of the key competencies at the intermediate level and specialist titles intended for particular tests such as those for the police, fire service or UK Civil Service. In each chapter I have suggested sources of further material.

Undertake two sorts of practice

Type 1

Practise on realistic questions in a relaxed situation without time constraint. The aim is to become really familiar with the types of question and to realize what skills are being examined. Take one question at a time, looking at the answer and any explanation. If you get any wrong, try to understand why. Use this time to recognize which part of the test represents the greatest challenge for you and use this information to plan the amount of practice you need to undertake for each part of the test. Spend most time on your personal areas of weakness.

Type 2

Once you feel confident in each of the types of question that you face, start practising on realistic questions under strict time constraints and under realistic exam-type conditions. You can make up these 'mock tests' by taking 40 questions and allowing yourself 25 minutes to attempt them. Use a watch to time yourself strictly and be sure to stop when you have run out of time. Even get someone to administer the test for you, telling you when to turn over the page and begin and to stop when you have run out of time. If you don't find your first mock test much of a challenge then either increase the number of questions or reduce the time you allow yourself. The aim of this second sort of practice is to get used to answering the questions under the pressure of time and to build up your speed and accuracy. Take this practice seriously, try to make every point count and work very quickly against what should feel like a tight time limit.

Set yourself a personal challenge

To get the most out of your practice and to help make it feel more realistic, set yourself the challenge of trying to beat your own score each time you take a mock test. To do this you will have to try hard and take the challenge seriously, and then you will have to try harder still. Try the following 10-step approach:

1. Become test wise and undertake the type 1 familiarization practice described above.

2. Make up three mock tests for each of the sub-tests that you face.

3. Take the first test under exam-type conditions and against a tight time constraint.

4. Mark your test and go over the questions you got wrong, working out why; if you did not finish the test then resolve to work faster next time. Record the number of answers you got right in the first box below.

5. Set yourself the challenge of beating your first score, get yourself in the right frame of mind and be ready to 'really go for it' in your second mock test.

6. Take your second mock test, making sure it contains the same number of questions and allowing yourself the same amount of time. Mark your answers, record your score and see if you did in fact beat your first score.

7. Go over the answers and explanations to your second test and, if you got any wrong, work out why.

8. Take a third test, trying once again to beat your best score.

9. Record your third score and go over any questions you may have got wrong.

10. Repeat this challenge for each of the sub-tests that make up the real test you face.

Record of mock test scores

Title of mock test _____

Test 1

[ ]

Test 2

[ ]

Test 3

[ ]

Copy this page to ensure that you can record your score in each sub-test.

The winning mindset

Doing well in a psychometric test takes practice but also the right mental approach. The winning candidate looks forward to the test. They have long ago left behind any sense of resentment or irritation. Instead they treat the test as an opportunity to show just how good they have become. So put aside any negative thoughts. They will not help. Focus on the opportunity that passing the test will afford you. Decide how much you want that opportunity and resolve to set about getting it.

It will take courage to make the necessary commitment, especially if you have previously experienced failure. But you must decide to take the risk! The winning candidate has committed everything to passing. They are fully prepared to risk not passing because they have concluded they have nothing to lose and everything to gain.

Adopt this uncompromising commitment both before the test when practising and during the test itself. Test administrators can often tell which candidates are going to do well. Typically the strongest candidate can't wait for the test to start. They work incredibly hard during the test and make every second count. They are test wise and very well prepared. They never forget why they are there. They attempt every question, which means they don't slow down or reflect for too long on any one question. When the questions are easy they maximize their speed while gaining every mark. When they are more difficult their preparation really begins to pay off. They have addressed their personal challenges and worked out beforehand how to deal with many of the more difficult questions and when they reach some they cannot answer they sparingly apply educated guessing. They never give up. When they are told to stop they feel truly exhausted from the mental effort.

What to do if you fail

If you are reading this book having failed a psychometric test and this has prevented you from realizing a career goal then take heart. It is entirely normal for candidates to fail on the first few attempts at many of the more popular tests. It certainly does not mean that you do not have the ability to do the job or course in question. However, it does mean that you need to improve on your performance in the test used to recruit to that position.

Failure will not mean that the company will not welcome a future application from you. Should you be successful at a later stage, once you are employed you will be judged by your performance in the job, not your past test scores, so it will not impinge on your future career prospects within the organization.

It is likely that over half the candidates who sit a psychometric test will fail. If this happens to you then ask the organization to provide you with feedback on your score and identify the parts of the test that you had problems with. Recall and note down the types of question, how many there were and the level of difficulty. Be honest with yourself and try to assess what it is that you need to do in order to pass next time.

I know candidates who repeatedly failed a test and it was only when they set about a major programme of improving their maths or English or both that they then went on to pass. Others simply needed to get more used to the test and working under pressure of time in an exam-type situation. It is not uncommon for accomplished applicants to fail a test because they think too long about the questions or read the passages too deeply. Their work or study does not well prepare them for a test in which you have to act very quickly to complete all the questions in the given time.

Plan a programme of revision and improvement straight away, concentrating on what you are least good at. Seek out sufficient practice material and get down to some seriously hard work.

Apply again as soon as you are able and, this time, attend fully prepared and confident in your abilities.

It will take courage and determination to try again and to keep working to improve yourself until you pass. But these are qualities of which you can be proud. With the right approach you will address your personal challenges and go on to pass. You will then be able to look back on what you can regard as a significant achievement.

May I take this opportunity to wish you every success in the psychometric test that you face.

3

Verbal Reasoning

By building your vocabulary and relearning the rules of usage you can significantly improve your score in these common tests. The practice provided in this chapter will mean that you approach the test on the day with greater confidence, speed and accuracy.

A verbal reasoning test features in most psychometric test batteries. They are used to test your vocabulary, comprehension and command of the rules of usage called grammar.

This chapter includes practice questions on most styles of question. Hundreds of examples are provided, affording many hours of practice. Set aside sufficient time to work through these questions and you will significantly improve your performance in these common tests.

Be prepared for different types of question as you work through the practice material. They are there to keep you on your toes and make sure you are prepared for every eventuality.

If you don't already have one, buy a dictionary and thesaurus and get into the habit of using them on a daily basis. Read a quality paper whenever you can, perhaps when commuting to work or at the weekend.

You can find further practice questions of this sort in other titles in the Kogan Page Testing Series.

At the intermediate level

How to Pass Selection Tests, 3rd edition, Mike Bryon and Sanjay Modha
How to Pass Verbal Reasoning Tests, 2nd edition, Harry Tolley and Ken Thomas

At a more advanced level

How to Pass Graduate Psychometric Tests, 2nd edition, Mike Bryon

Also CD ROM, *Psychometric Tests Volume 1*, The Times Testing Series

Word link

Find two words, one from each list, closest in meaning or with the strongest connection.

1. A. Bargain   D. Property
    B. Purchase   E. Acquisition   Answer ☐
    C. Leverage   F. Positive

2. A. Recognition   D. Acknowledgement
    B. Denial   E. Reckon   Answer ☐
    C. Ignore   F. Acquaintance

3. A. Fashionable   D. Dejected
    B. Liable   E. Blame   Answer ☐
    C. Counsel   F. Accountable

4. A. Constant   D. Variable
    B. Valuable   E. Ridged   Answer ☐
    C. Flexible   F. Flow

5. A. Resentment   D. Attachment
    B. Embarrassment   E. Argument   Answer ☐
    C. Supplement   F. Statement

6. A. Adapt   D. Obscure
    B. Observe   E. Respect   Answer ☐
    C. Believe   F. Disregard

7. A. Jagged   D. Affected
    B. Justified   E. Competing   Answer ☐
    C. Adjoining   F. Juxtaposed

8. A. Suspension   D. Instruction
    B. Hasten   E. Disappointment   Answer ☐
    C. Intentional   F. Deferral

9. A. Discriminate   D. Negotiate
    B. Cultivate   E. Generate   Answer ☐
    C. Arbitrate   F. Initiate

10. A. Fix   D. Concoct
    B. Secure   E. Rectify   Answer ☐
    C. Expose   F. Trouble

11. A. Governing Body   D. Advise
    B. Counsel   E. Authority   Answer ☐
    C. Delegate   F. Advocate

(note it is common in this type of question for more than one pair
of the suggested answers to have connections, you must select the
two words with the closest connection)

12. A. Itemize   D. Glance
    B. Observe   E. Sketch   Answer ☐
    C. Outline   F. Explain

13. A. Serious   D. Expedient
    B. Beneficial   E. Benevolent   Answer ☐
    C. Favourite   F. Favourable

14. A. Willing   D. Overbearing
    B. Considerate   E. Wretched   Answer ☐
    C. Oppressive   F. Immerse

15. A. Prime   D. Prior
    B. Pride   E. Procedure   Answer ☐
    C. Preceding   F. Subsequent

Word link – synonyms

In the following style of word link questions you are again looking for the two words closest in meaning or with the strongest connection. Such words are called synonyms.

16. Corporate is to conglomerate as:

    focus is to   A. diverge   Answer

                           B. aim

                           C. fringe

17. Observant is to vigilant as:

    align is to   A. disembark   Answer

                           B. fondness

                           C. affiliate

18. Symbolic is to metaphorical as:

    all is to   A. every   Answer

                           B. the

                           C. of

19. Alleviate is to mitigate as:

    adverse is to   A. opponent   Answer

                           B. fortunate

                           C. ill-starred

20. Nullify is to quash as:

    insincerity is to   A. platitudes   Answer

                           B. genuine

                           C. forthright

21. Relent is to acquiesce as:

    remiss is to   A. diligent   Answer

                           B. sensible

                           C. imprudent

22. Rebuke is to reprimand as:

    contingent is to   A. fortuitous   Answer ☐

                          B. deliberate

                          C. incidental

23. Genre is to class as:

    obsolete is to   A. modern   Answer ☐

                          B. outmoded

                          C. watchful

24. Deceit is to fraud as:

    decision is to   A. conclusion   Answer ☐

                          B. solve

                          C. indecision

25. Uphold is to sustain as:

    magnitude is to   A. infinitive   Answer ☐

                          B. charm

                          C. proportion

26. Announce is to declare as:

    characterize is to   A. disposition   Answer ☐

                          B. portray

                          C. distinguished

27. Objective is to goal as:

    judge is to   A. punish   Answer ☐

                          B. appraise

                          C. forensic

28. Co-ordinate is to harmonize as:

    commodity is to   A. primary product   Answer ☐

                          B. brown goods

                          C. bonds

29. Responsive is to elastic as:

    rival is to   A. colleague   Answer
                   B. partner
                   C. competitor

30. Manufacture is to production as:

    lease is to   A. agreement   Answer
                   B. ownership
                   C. liberate

31. Niche is to segment as:

    perks are to   A. deductions   Answer
                   B. benefits
                   C. taxation

32. Train is to teach as:

    services are to A. utilities Answer
                     B. churches
                     C. commodities

33. Amount is to volume as:

    abrupt is to   A. courteous   Answer
                   B. private
                   C. brusque

34. Get back is to return as:

    distribute is to A. collect   Answer
                      B. allocate
                      C. manage

Word link – opposites

This style of word link question requires you to identify the suggested answer that means the opposite of the word on the left.

35. Ascend   A. Surmount
                  B. Escalate   Answer ☐
                  C. Descend

36. Scornful   A. Jovial
                  B. Mocking   Answer ☐
                  C. Sneering

37. Warrant   A. Authorize
                  B. Prohibit   Answer ☐
                  C. Ratify

38. Shrewd   A. Foolish
                  B. Discerning   Answer ☐
                  C. Intelligent

39. Plummet   A. Decline
                  B. Rise   Answer ☐
                  C. Falter

40. Tortuous   A. Safeguard
                  B. Meandering   Answer ☐
                  C. Direct
                  D. Devious

41. Aggravate   A. Vex
                  B. Annoy   Answer ☐
                  C. Pacify

42. Annul   A. Confirm
                  B. Rescind   Answer ☐
                  C. Cancel

43. Respect
    A. Admire
    B. Despise   Answer ☐
    C. Exalt

44. Relapse
    A. Recede
    B. Progress   Answer ☐
    C. Retreat
    D. Worsen

45. Arrest
    A. Impede
    B. Hinder   Answer ☐
    C. Check
    D. Accelerate

46. Unfaltering
    A. Courageous
    B. Irresolute   Answer ☐
    C. Inflexible
    D. Adamant

47. Replenish
    A. Restock
    B. Stock   Answer ☐
    C. Exhaust
    D. Provide

48. Answer
    A. Echo
    B. Reply   Answer ☐
    C. Question
    D. Respond

49. Lucrative
    A. Unprofitable
    B. Unlimited   Answer ☐
    C. Advantageous

50. Exact
    A. Conscientious
    B. Lax   Answer ☐
    C. Advantageous

51. Counter   A. Confirm
                      B. Rebut   Answer [   ]
                      C. Deny

52. Purified   A. Pure
                      B. Clarified   Answer [   ]
                      C. Crude
                      D. Refined

53. Right   A. Amend
                      B. Redress   Answer [   ]
                      C. Remedy
                      D. Wrong

54. Distraction   A. Amusement
                      B. Work   Answer [   ]
                      C. Pastime
                      D. Hobby

55. Sway   A. Deter
                      B. Entice   Answer [   ]
                      C. Allure
                      D. Coax

56. Steep is to gradual as:
     bicker is to   A. agree   Answer [   ]
                      B. wrangle
                      C. scrap

57. Solemn is to frivolous as:
     rudimentary is to A. basic   Answer [   ]
                        B. sophisticated
                        C. fundamental

58. Cower is to stand as:

    devastating is to   A. damaging   Answer ☐
                         B. cataclysmic
                         C. beneficial

59. Contend is to agree as:

    scramble is to   A. scurry   Answer ☐
                         B. dawdle
                         C. sprint

60. Disdain is to respect as:

    disseminate is to   A. collect   Answer ☐
                         B. broadcast
                         C. disperse

61. Incentive is to deterrent as:

    terrific is to   A. rich   Answer ☐
                         B. poor
                         C. marvellous

62. Impromptu is to rehearsed as:

    audit is to   A. inspect   Answer ☐
                         B. scrutinize
                         C. ignore

63. Particular is to general as:

    speculation is to   A. reality   Answer ☐
                         B. surmise
                         C. hypothesis

64. Alleviate is to irritate as:

    disagreeable is to   A. repulsion   Answer ☐
                         B. pleasant
                         C. nastiness

65. Complicate is to clarify as:

    busy is to   A. slack   Answer ☐
                        B. limp
                        C. lax

66. Memorable is to ordinary as:

    tortuous is to   A. devious   Answer ☐
                        B. meandering
                        C. direct

67. Divulge is to conceal as:

    percentage is to   A. fraction   Answer ☐
                        B. whole
                        C. decimal

68. Savage is to mild as:

    tangible is to   A. insensitive   Answer ☐
                        B. appreciable
                        C. imperceptible

69. Different is to corresponding as:

    superior is to   A. elder   Answer ☐
                        B. junior
                        C. manager

70. Presently is to later as:

    infrequently is to A. scarcely   Answer ☐
                        B. seldom
                        C. often

71. Captivity is to freedom as:

    fit is to   A. compulsive   Answer ☐
                        B. competent
                        C. incapacitated

72. Disgrace is to honour as:

   alarmist is to   A. optimist   Answer ☐

                     B. scaremonger

                     C. outright

73. Eminent is to unknown as:

   descendant is to   A. accent   Answer ☐

                     B. ancestor

                     C. family

Find the new word

In this type of verbal reasoning test you must find a four-letter word or words that is made up from the end of one of the given words and the beginning of the next.

Worked example

74. lumpy   swea**t**   **our**selves   Answer | tour |

75. anthropoid   learning   peppery   Answer ☐

76. welcome   guarantee   muddle   Answer ☐

77. result   motivation   lyric   Answer ☐

78. handlebar   identify   succulent   Answer ☐

79. recharge   nephew   handful   Answer ☐

80. nature   lyric   composer   Answer ☐

81. alcohol   swear   charcoal   Answer ☐

82. glorify   tormentil   tutor   Answer [____]

83. hour   geology   rescind   Answer [____]

84. unearth   overhear   library   Answer [____]

85. offspring   incision   toxic   Answer [____]

86. gastric   humane   engage   Answer [____]

87. ashore   airline   archer   Answer [____]

88. lapse   multi-media   lifeboat   Answer [____]

89. Hindu   typical   peddle   Answer [____]

90. reserve   proposal   electricity   Answer [____]

91. defuse   education   voyage   Answer [____]

92. flatter   muscle   scream   Answer [____]

93. jaded   piano   teaspoon   Answer [____]

94. jersey   elliptical   monster   Answer [____]

95. cockroach   aplomb   winkle   Answer [____]

96. insult   ignore   alternate   Answer [____]

97. monumental   epidemic   fortify   Answer [   ]

98. taste   arduous   season   Answer [   ]

99. staff   lagoon   scuffle   Answer [   ]

100. contest   scientific   ultimate   Answer [   ]

101. flotsam   epicentre   anonymous   Answer [   ]

102. effigy   enzyme   aluminium   Answer [   ]

103. rumpus   habit   tension   Answer [   ]

104. siphon   lyric   notebook   Answer [   ]

105. wobbly   echo   petrol   Answer [   ]

106. amoeba   nervous   rummage   Answer [   ]

107. conjuror   parabola   stringy   Answer [   ]

108. litmus   throttle   needle   Answer [   ]

109. hypnotize   rough   scribble   Answer [   ]

110. aurora   censure   official   Answer [   ]

111. altogether   momentum   alternate   Answer [   ]

112. ideal   lynch   senior   Answer

113. windfall   mask   incapable   Answer

114. into   negotiate   hoist   Answer

115. underline   mode   afraid   Answer

116. envelop   almighty   rumour   Answer

117. island   miscellaneous   thwart   Answer

118. physical   American   inedible   Answer

119. helmet   charcoal   selfish   Answer

120. normal   prig   asphalt   Answer

121. international   usherette   apartment   Answer

122. wrestle   maybe   statute   Answer

123. commonwealth   athletic   nonsense   Answer

124. also   urgent   inventor   Answer

Word swap

Each of the following questions comprises a sentence in which two words need to be interchanged to make it read sensibly. Only swap two words so that one replaces the other.

125. Don't try to be yourself else, be someone.

Answer [   ]

126. Breaking up to hard is do.

Answer [   ]

127. Squabbles is so often the root of family money.

Answer [   ]

128. Every American of generation has thought itself more stressed out than the last.

Answer [   ]

129. Sometimes these remedies can result remarkably quickly, with a positive work occurring within hours.

Answer [   ]

130. As steady she goes.

Answer [   ]

131. We met in a city in the heart of the café of Milan.

Answer [   ]

132. Book publishing is big business, the industry is worth £4 billion and more than 12,000 books are published in the UK a year and each third of which are exported.

Answer [   ]

133. The spokeswoman for the company 'Archrival' said it would give a board and shareholders of 'Goodbuy' the further two weeks to consider its improved takeover bid.

      Answer [   ]

134. A two-hour drive of 200 kilometres from the motorway on Milan would bring you to the Mediterranean Sea.

      Answer [   ]

135. Reporting to the Chief Accountant the challenging candidate will work in a successful environment providing high-level economic analysis on diverse, key industrial issues.

      Answer [   ]

136. Good employees establish unity of purpose and direction among the leaders of an organization.

      Answer [   ]

137. We know evolution happens because of a convergence of evidence from developed fields of science, together they reveal that life diverse driven by the process of natural selection.

      Answer [   ]

138. People will be better motivated and understand the organization goals and objectives if miscommunication between the levels of an organization's are avoided.

      Answer [   ]

139. The distances to remote galaxies are increasing and this inflation can be explained with an analogy of the expansion of a balloon.

      Answer [   ]

140. A fuel cell powered car is an electric supplied vehicle with effectively a refuelable battery that keeps generating electricity so long as hydrogen and oxygen are powered.

      Answer [   ]

141. A new hypothesis puts forward the human view that global warming in fact started thousands of years before the industrial revolution caused by unfashionable deforestation and farming.

    Answer [   ]

142. The scene of the rich at play could be played out anywhere in the world, the vase of orchids, a man in a bar speaking into a mobile phone, laughter from the suit and an elegantly dressed woman checking in at reception.

    Answer [   ]

143. Paula wrote that American bull markets were long over due a correction as they were in her opinion greatly overvalued after the longest financial market in economic history.

    Answer [   ]

144. As far as economic management is concerned he was very lucky to inherit what he did, growth had already fallen and inflation had returned, importantly, the lessons of the deep recession had been learnt.

    Answer [   ]

145. France's National Assembly approved a constitutional treaty to allow for the referendum on the European Union's constitutional change and a date for the referendum was set for 2005.

    Answer [   ]

146. Last year's records from England and Wales suggest that marriage is still more popular than divorce as 57,000 couples were married against 150,000 divorced.

    Answer [   ]

147. Drive into Liverpool from Manchester and the route of economic dereliction that once dominated the signs are now almost all gone.

    Answer [   ]

148. Speaking on his mobile phone he would argue, pour and romantic secrets out talk so loudly that everyone on the bus would find it hard not to listen.

    Answer [   ]

149. The most important tenet of foreign policy for America is to maintain good relations with its powerful neighbour and most dominant trading partner Mexico.

Answer [   ]

150. Comparisons between India and China are tempting because they are both large agricultural societies that are undergoing economic development at a fantastic rate but China is fundamentally an open society while India is still intolerant of dissent.

Answer [   ]

151. Manufacturing has spread from its origins of setting up and running a company's IT systems and now provides a multitude of services including finance, accounting, human resources, design and even outsourcing.

Answer [   ]

Sentence sequencing

Your task in this style of question is to reorganize the sentences into the order in which they were originally written.

152. A. Pluto is the ninth and the most distant from the sun. B. It is tiny compared with the giants Jupiter, Saturn, Neptune and Uranus which have massive, dense, gaseous atmospheres. C. Our solar system has nine planets formed from gas and dust left over after the sun was formed.

Answer [   ]

153. A. The best farmland and industries are concentrated in the north which is mountainous and has a cool wet climate. B. The mainland peninsula and the island of Sicily and Sardinia make up the country. C. The dryer, hotter south relies more on farming and tourism than industry and has active volcanoes.

Answer [   ]

154. A. This is pollution. B. It can be small-scale or global and most plants and animals suffer its effects. C. Harmful by-products of industry and agriculture enter the environment.

Answer [   ]

155. A. Large buildings have foundations which form the base on which they are constructed. B. They all tend to have a roof, walls and a floor. C. Buildings come in a huge variety of sizes and shapes from tower blocks and super-markets to garden sheds. D. Despite the differences they all serve the same purpose of providing shelter for us and our belongings.

Answer

156. A. Food is important in other ways too. B. Anything that we can digest is food. C. We get our energy and essential bodily nourishment from what we eat. D. Because not having enough, the right sort or eating too much leads to bad health.

Answer

157. A. The rapid growth in urban living has been largely unplanned. B. By contrast, today half the world's population lives in cities. C. As a consequence, inadequate housing and an absence of essential amenities are common. D. Two hundred years ago most people lived in villages or small towns.

Answer

158. A. It protects us from the most harmful of the sun's rays and retains the sun's heat. B. The earth is surrounded by colourless and odourless gases. C. They are mainly nitrogen and oxygen but also carbon dioxide and a gas called argon. D. Without this atmosphere life on the planet would not be possible.

Answer

159. A. Plastics have become the most used material in the world. B. The exception is rubber, a naturally occurring plastic extracted from trees. C. Their molecules are made up of very long chains of atoms. D. Most are synthetic, made from chemicals extracted from oil.

Answer

160. A. However, while muscles can pull they cannot push; for this reason most movements rely on a pair of muscles pulling in opposite directions. B. One end is connected to a bone that does not move and the other to one that does. C. We can move because our muscles contract. D. When the muscle contracts it pulls the moving bone.

Answer

161. A. It is readily exchanged for goods as long as the buyer and seller both accept its value. B. They may only be made from common metals and paper but they are accepted as valuable because of what they represent. C. Money works as a 'standard of value'. D. The most familiar forms of money are coins and banknotes.

Answer [   ]

162. A. It is produced by vibrations that travel by moving molecules which bump into one another. B. In air sound travels at over 300 metres per second. C. Sound is a form of energy. D. These vibrations are called sound waves.

Answer [   ]

163. A. Frames are constructed rising from the foundations. B. The building site is cleared and levelled. C. The interior is decorated. D. Foundations are built by pouring concrete into the holes. E. Services are installed on each floor. F. Excavations are made for foundations and basements.

Answer [   ]

164. A. The findings of a study concluded that three-quarters of taxpayers pay too much tax. B. It was claimed that taxpayers will pay more than £5 billion in unnecessary taxes next year. C. Their investigations found that the vast majority of taxpayers take no action to reduce the amount of tax that they pay. D. The authors urged taxpayers to take the trouble to claim refunds and reliefs to which they are entitled.

Answer [   ]

165. A. Iron is by far the most used by mankind. B. To produce iron its ore is mixed with coal and limestone and heated to high temperatures in a furnace. C. There are more than 50 metals found naturally as ores. D. This produces pig iron which is further refined to make steel.

Answer [   ]

166.   A. The system is interactive. B. A travel agency illustrates well how telecom-
       munications and computers are used to improve customer service. C. This
       means that when an employee wants to access the system he or she enters data
       and the system replies with further screens until the desired outcome is
       realized. D. The agency uses an online enquiry and booking service from a
       terminal in the office that is connected to a remote server by a telecommunica-
       tions link.

       Answer [   ]

167.   A. The home page is usually the first thing that you will see when you first
       access a site. B. Each website has its own unique address which is called its
       uniform resource locator. C. It is divided into millions of sites which are files
       made up of pages of information. D. Perhaps the most significant service
       available on the internet is the World Wide Web.

       Answer [   ]

168.   A. There are thought to be billions of them. B. Perhaps the most common objects
       in the universe are stars. C. It includes everything visible, invisible, known and
       not yet known. D. The universe is made up of everything that exists.

       Answer [   ]

169.   A. It involves the temporary, voluntary movement of people. B. It is estimated
       that one in ten of the working population is engaged in the industry. C. Affected
       are the places and people through which they pass and the people who make
       the trip possible. D. Tourism is the fasting-growing industry in the world today.

       Answer [   ]

170.   A. But most of the population live in the much milder south. B. It occupies the
       Scandinavian peninsular with Norway. C. Twenty-five per cent of the
       country lies within the bitterly cold artic circle. D. Sweden is the fifth largest
       country in Europe.

       Answer [   ]

171. A. Reformers want new laws that will make the owners of casinos act in socially responsible ways. B. These tricks might include removing clocks from the gambling floor, simulating daylight and making the exit hard to find. C. The new super casinos will be something completely new and some fear that they will deploy psychological techniques to maximize gambling. D. In particular, they want regulations that ban the casino operators from encouraging people to gamble or that increase the risk of problem gambling.

Answer

172. A. 'It is a great disappointment to find young employees so deficient in their command of English', wrote one. B. Reading is one of the most important keys to success. C. But what is happening to standards? D. Employers are critical.

Answer

173. A. From the road you just glimpse the tops of the houses with names such as Sweet View and Ocean Swell. B. It boasts a cinema, tennis court, two pools and elegant but informal gardens and terraces that all look out to sea. C. Inside the high walls and closed gates of the two and a half hectare site you begin to appreciate the extent to which it caters for the lifestyle of the extremely wealthy.

Answer

174. A. The very hot coolant is used to generate steam to drive turbines and produce electricity. B. A nuclear power station uses the energy produced by a controlled nuclear reaction. C. A series of chain reactions occur inside the core and produce heat. D. The heat is carried away by a coolant circulating the core.

Answer

175. A. The fairytale writer is its most famous adopted daughter. B. She gave the world classics such as *The Lost Teddy Bear* and *The Adventures of Young Tom*. C. The centenary of Lisa Smith approaches and the city of Leeds plans many celebrations. D. Adopted because she was not born there but made it her home for over three decades.

Answer

176. A. Therefore keeping the walls warm can save heat. B. Office managers who leave the heating on over weekends report lower annual fuel bills than if they turn the heating off at these times. C. This has been proven in several academic studies and is supported by considerable anecdotal evidence. D. When heating is turned on in a cold building a lot of heat is first used to evaporate condensed moisture in the walls.

Answer [   ]

Best word(s) to complete a sentence

These questions comprise a sentence with one or more pairs of suggested words from which you must choose the one that correctly completes the sentence.

177. If the courts make insurance companies pay liabilities/compensation on claims for asymptomatic conditions then premiums must be expected to rise sharply.

Answer [   ]

178. According to industrial sources Castle Cole, the property company, is performing/perfume in line with expectations at the operating level/cycle.

Answer [   ]

179. Macleans, the London insurer, was on tract/track to meet full-year expectations the/with future performance underpinned by its successful new savings product.

Answer [   ]

180. A rescue plan for Village Leisure, the failing/falling media company, was agreed by shareholders at an extraordinary meeting/moratorium.

Answer [   ]

181. A/The biggest utility company in the new EU member countries reported that its recent perpetuity/promotional activities had failed to have the desired impact.

Answer [   ]

182. Strikes escalated as/at the Guy company yesterday after a third round of negotiations with unions failed to reach a commodity/compromise.

Answer [   ]

183. The chancellor faced revenue/renewed demands to avoid further increases for/in the tax burden on companies in the forthcoming budget report.

    Answer

184. Output in Britain's factories rallied/depreciated as strong demand from/to China and South East Asia boosted exports.

    Answer

185. Manufacturing growth of/in the Eurozone dwindled to its lowest level in 12 months as a result of high oil prices and a slowing/deprecating global economy.

    Answer

186. Continuing price competition and higher utility and labour costs resulted in/from a second quarter decline in the group's net operating margins/accruals.

    Answer

187. British firms have failed to/in implement government recommendations about investing in and managing their workforces because they have been busy responding/adjusting to unprecedented regulatory changes.

    Answer

188. Forty per cent of the total cost base is commissions or bonuses, making it frequently/comparatively easy for costs to be slashed when/if demand shrinks; offices are on short-term leases, again giving flexibility to cut back at short notice.

    Answer

189. The litigation/strategy fits with the practice of mining a diversified set of related revenue seams, hopefully giving the business a broader and more solid form/from from/form which to build profits.

    Answer

190. The company is in the midst of a growth spurt/opportunity cost, funded through a reversible/convertible bond, to expand and diversify its portfolio of business activities.

    Answer

191. Based on/in new data collected last year, the actuarial/actors profession estimates hundreds of thousands more asbestos-related insurance/malicious claims over the next 30 years.

    Answer [   ]

192. The miscellaneous/media regulator has decreed that advertisements must not link alcohol with sexual attractiveness or success or imply that alcohol can enhance attractiveness, or/nor may the commercial/memorandum refer to daring tough or unruly behaviour.

    Answer [   ]

193. Flotation/cautious trading ahead of the imminent election meant that markets were especially quiet. Volumes were more akin/like to those at Christmas with investors reluctant to take up large positions/permutations ahead of the outcome of the ballot.

    Answer [   ]

194. Europe's ageing population will be able/unable to sustain the cost of maintaining pensions for its growing number of pensioners because economic growth will stagnate and institutions will be faced with contraction/contradictions and decline/abatement.

    Answer [   ]

195. Eurozone GDP growth is/while still weak which is discouraging for UK exporters to the region, but US GDP growth/market is stronger than has been expected and UK interest rates/fluctuations are likely to increase only slowly.

    Answer [   ]

196. Results/measures of companies' expectations of orders, sales and profitability show the extremely/theoretical sharp drop in confidence in the wake of the terrorist attacks in the United States followed by the strong return of confidence last June and then a trailing off during the remaining/previous months.

    Answer [   ]

English usage

This style of question comprises a sentence with some words missing and suggested lists from which you must choose the answer that correctly completes the sentence.

197.   __A___ the animals in the park while we were ___B___ behind the tree.

A	B
1. We saw	1. sitting
2. We see	2. sit
3. Seeing	3. sat

Answer [   ]

198.   Which of the following words can be a preposition?

A. location

B. no

C. in

D. position

Answer [   ]

199.   I __A__ call because I had __B__ my telephone.

A	B
1. can't	1. forgotten
2. couldn't	2. forget
3. could	3. forgetting
4. can	

Answer [   ]

200.   Which of the following is a superlative?

A. large

B. larger

C. largest

Answer [   ]

201.   Children please don't make so much noise. __A__.

A

1. I am concentrating.

2. I concentrate.

3. While I concentrate

Answer [   ]

202. Which word is the past participle?

The broken marriage was a great disappointment to all.

Answer [   ]

203. My mother is in hospital. I went to __A__ to visit her. My brother is at __B__ now.

A	B
1. the hospital	1. hospital
2. hospital	2. the hospital

Answer [   ]

204. As I get __A__ I find myself getting ___B___.

A	B
1. more old	1. seriouser
2. older	2. more serious

Answer [   ]

205. When I __A__ Sam last night he was out __B__ in the park.

A	B
1. call	1. run
2. calling	2. ran
3. called	3. running

Answer [   ]

206. Which word is the noun?

'Good ideas sometimes occur slowly.'

Answer [   ]

207. Two thousand euros __A__ found in the waste paper bin.

A. is

B. was

C. were

D. are

Answer [   ]

208. Which adjective is the comparative?

A. late

B. later

C. latest

Answer [   ]

209. The apartment was expensive but not __A__ expensive __B__ the first one
      we viewed.

      A   B
      1. so   1. as   Answer [   ]
      2. as   2. so

210. The oldest person __A__ the world also lives the __B__ from a doctor.

      A   B
      1. of   1. most far
      2. in   2. furthest   Answer [   ]
      3. farthest

211. You __A__ earn a fortune to __B__ such an expensive house.

      A   B
      1. mustn't   1. live in
      2. might   2. lived
      3. can't   3. living   Answer [   ]
      4. must   4. lived in
      5. can

212. Which is the verb?

      Cleaning the bookshelves was done every Tuesday.

                                                     Answer [   ]

213. I __A__ animals __B__ I prefer them to people.

      A   B
      1. like very much   1. very much and
      2. like   2. and   Answer [   ]
      3. very much

214. With the cancellation the exhibition would __A__ longer be sold out but
      anyway it is not on ___B___ longer.

      A   B
      1. any   1. no   Answer [   ]
      2. no   2. any

215. I __A__ a lot of films when I __B__ a teenager.

    A   B

    1. watched   1. wasn't

    2. have watched   2. am   Answer

    3. watching   3. was

216. He left late yet __A__ the fact that it was very cold and in __B__ the snow he still got there early.

    A   B

    1. despite of   1. spite of   Answer

    2. despite   2. spite

217. I hope to visit the church __A__.

    A

    1. while I am there

    2. while I will be there   Answer

    3. while I am their

218. I was given __A__ ten __B__ notes for my three __C__ work.

    A   B   C

    1. a   1. pound   1. hour

    2. one   2. pounds   2. hours   Answer

    3. two

219. My wife will be away __A__ Sunday __B__ which time we will have finished the work.

    A   B

    1. until   1. by   Answer

    2. by   2. until

220. Neil Armstrong walked on the moon __A__ 3 am __B__ a Saturday __C__ July 1969.

    A   B   C

    1. at   1. in   1. on

    2. on   2. on   2. in   Answer

    3. in   3. at   3. at

221. We __A__ for __B__ so much noise.

A   B

1. apologize   1. make

2. apology   2. making   Answer ☐

3. apologized   3. made

222. The __A__ was in the __B__.

A   B

1. childs bag   1. back of the car

2. child's bag   2. car's back   Answer ☐

3. bag of the child   3. car back

223. The journey to the party involved getting __A__ a plane, __B__ a car, __C__ a
      bicycle and at last I arrived __D__ the party.

A   B   C   D

1. on   1. on   1. on   1. on

2. in   2. in   2. in   2. in   Answer ☐

3. at   3. at   3. at   3. at

Identify the correct sentence or word(s)

What follows is a mix of question styles including questions that offer a number of
sentences of which only one or none is correct in terms of English usage.

224. Which sentence if any contains an error?

A. Before the meeting he greeted both the Company Secretary and the
   Finance Director.

B. Before the meeting he greeted the Company Secretary and Finance
   Director.

C. Neither is correct.

Answer ☐

225. Which sentences if any contain an error?

   A. Bart usually drove real careful but the Police Officer was unimpressed that he had both broken the speed limit and jumped the red light.

   B. Bart usually drove really carefully but the Police Officer was both unimpressed that he had broken the speed limit and jumped the red light.

   C. Bart usually drove really carefully but the Police Officer was unimpressed that he had broken the speed limit and jumped a red light.

   D. None is correct.

   Answer ☐

226. __A__ friend is a friend of __B__.

   A   B
   1. you   1. mine
   2. yours   2. me
   3. your

   Answer ☐

227. Indicate which if any of the following sentences contain an error.

   A. The five children really enjoyed the show and was happy to share the sweets among them.

   B. The five children really enjoyed the show and were happy to share the sweets between them.

   C. The five children really enjoyed the show and were happy to share the sweets among them.

   D. None is correct.

   Answer ☐

228. They were seen __A__ to the kitchen just before I __B__ something burning in the kitchen.

   A   B
   1. to go   1. smelt
   2. going   2. smell
   3. smelling

   Answer ☐

229. We had a lovely holiday __A__ Sardinia and spent the last day __B__ the beach.

   A   B
   1. in   1. in
   2. on   2. on
   3. at   3. at

   Answer ☐

230. Which is the adjective?

    The slow car stopped.   Answer [   ]

231. My sister and I have three brothers, two of __A__ are left handed.

    A
    1. them
    2. they   Answer [   ]
    3. which

232. He could not decide if he was __A__ experienced or if he wasn't experienced __B__.

    A   B
    1. enough   1. too
    2. to   2. to   Answer [   ]
    3. too   3. enough

233. I was sitting __A__ the bus when we saw David __B__ the back of the building.

    A   B
    1. in   1. in
    2. at   2. at   Answer [   ]
    3. on   3. on

234. Which part of the sentence is the continuous present tense?

    I am doing my best.
                                                    Answer [   ]

235. They __A__ Italy on time but did not __B__ Rome until late and __C__ home in the early hours.

    A   B   C
    1. arrived   1. got to   1. arrived in
    2. arrived to   2. get   2. arrived to   Answer [   ]
    3. arrived in   3. get to   3. arrived

236. We drove there __A__ car. Can you remember whether or not we paid __B__ cheque or __C__ cash?

A	B	C	
1. in my	1. by	1. by	Answer
2. by my	2. in	2. in	

237. How many adjectives are in the sentence:

The beautiful young woman was wearing a blue and green dress.

Answer

238. How many of the following sentences contain an error?

A. The design was one of the most unique.

B. The design was the most unique.

C. The design was unique.

Answer

D. None.

239. It rained __A__ much and for __B__ long time.

A	B	
1. such	1. such	
2. so	2. so	Answer
	3. such a	

240. The man was wearing a __A__ coat.

A

1. long and red

2. red and long

3. long, red   Answer

4. long red

241. Peter is a good friend __A__ lives in Italy, a country __B__ I have never visited.

A	B	
1. who	1. what	
2. that	2. whom	Answer
3. and	3. which	
4. whom		

242. Which is a plural reflective pronoun?

    A. myself

    B. my

    C. ours

    D. mine   Answer [   ]

    E. yourself

    F. themselves

243. __A__ rugby team scored three kick goals.

    According to the timetable the train runs __B__ day twice __C__ hour.

A	B	C	
1. every	1. each	1. every	Answer [ ]
2. each	2. every	2. each	

244. With little money but __A__ time you can visit a __B__ museums.

A	B	
1. little	1. little	
2. much	2. much	Answer [ ]
3. few	3. few	

245. Tom is lazy and never has __A__ work while Joe always has __B__ work to do.

A	B	
1. some	1. any	Answer [ ]
2. any	2. some	

246. __A__ a new cinema opened in town but when I went __B__ was closed.

A	B	
1. It	1. there	
2. there	2. there's	Answer [ ]
3. their	3. it	
4. there's	4. their	

Read a passage and evaluate a statement

These questions provide a series of passages and statements that relate to them. It is your task to read the passage and decide if the statements are true, false or that you cannot tell if they are true or false. It is important to remember that in your decision you should rely only on the information provided in the passage.

If you find these questions easy then you may be allowing yourself too leisurely a read and too much time to answer the questions. In a real test situation you really only have time for one fast, careful read and you will have to work through the question very quickly; also, you may have to turn the page and so not have the passage to hand for cross-referencing. You may well also be suffering from anxiety. For realistic practice set yourself a strict time constraint and work quickly, to the point where you risk getting some questions wrong. That way you will develop a winning exam technique.

Passage 1

Light is made up of electromagnetic waves. These vary in length and it is these differences that we perceive as different colours. White light has all the wavelengths of the light spectrum mixed up together. An object looks coloured because light falls on it and it reflects only certain parts of the spectrum. The rest of the spectrum is absorbed by the object. An object that looks white reflects all the light that falls on it. An object that looks red reflects the red part of the spectrum and absorbs the rest. Our eyes detect these different reflected waves and we see them as different colours.

247.   Without colours we would consider the world a dull and less beautiful place.

   A. True

   B. False   Answer

   C. Cannot tell

248.   White light is an amalgam of all the wave lengths of light.

   A. True

   B. False   Answer

   C. Cannot tell

249.   The passage states that an object that looks blue absorbs all but the blue wavelengths of light.

   A. True

   B. False   Answer

   C. Cannot tell

250. The colour we perceive an object to be is determined by the electromagnetic waves that it absorbs or reflects.

    A. True
    B. False   Answer
    C. Cannot tell

251. White paint reflects more light than red paint.

    A. True
    B. False   Answer
    C. Cannot tell

Passage 2

Between 1797 and 1815 Europe went through the Napoleonic wars. This period saw France at war with the kingdoms of Prussia, Russia, Austria, Spain and Britain. At that time the French army was the most powerful in Europe. By 1808 France had conquered much of the continent and had created the largest European empire since the Romans two thousand years before. Napoleon Bonaparte was its emperor and the military leader who oversaw the many major victories. However, a disastrous campaign in Russia, retreat from the Spanish peninsular and British supremacy at sea eventually allowed a combined European force to defeat Napoleon's army at Waterloo.

252. The Napoleonic wars lasted 18 years.

    A. True
    B. False   Answer
    C. Cannot tell

253. By 1808 Napoleon headed an empire that controlled most of the continent of Europe.

    A. True
    B. False   Answer
    C. Cannot tell

254. At the height of Napoleon's victories the French army was the largest in Europe.

    A. True
    B. False   Answer
    C. Cannot tell

255. France won battles against Prussia, Russia, Austria and Britain.

   A. True

   B. False   Answer

   C. Cannot tell

256. The passage states that the battle of Waterloo took place in 1815.

   A. True

   B. False   Answer

   C. Cannot tell

Passage 3

Traditionally medicine was the science of curing illness with treatments. For thousands of years people would have used plants and would have turned to priests for cures. In more recent times illness has been attributed less to the intervention of gods or magic and instead to natural causes. Medicine today is as much concerned with prevention as cure. Doctors use treatments of many types, including radiation and vaccination, both of which were unknown until very recent times. Other treatments have been known about and practised for centuries. Muslim doctors were skilled surgeons and treated pain with opium. When Europeans first reach the Americas they found healers who used many plants to cure illnesses. The Europeans adopted many of these treatments and some are still effective and in use today.

257. Modern medicine is the science of curing illness.

   A. True

   B. False   Answer

   C. Cannot tell

258. Medicine is a science that owes its success to modern treatments.

   A. True

   B. False   Answer

   C. Cannot tell

259. Vaccination is a relatively recent discovery.

   A. True

   B. False   Answer

   C. Cannot tell

260. The author of the passage believes that prevention is better than cure.

    A. True

    B. False   Answer

    C. Cannot tell

261. Practitioners of modern medicine make use of many techniques and technologies.

    A. True

    B. False   Answer

    C. Cannot tell

Passage 4

Asia is the world's largest continent and stretches from the Baring Sea in the east to Turkey and Europe in the west. Its southern border comprises many islands, including those that make up Indonesia. Since independence of colonial powers Asian economies have boomed. First were Japan, Singapore, Taiwan and South Korea and later Malaysia, Thailand and Indonesia. More recently China and India have enjoyed rapid economic growth. The south-west and central parts of the continent are deserts. The Himalayan mountains divide the cold north from the tropical south. The people of Asia make up over two-thirds of the world's population and they live in the birthplace of the world's earliest civilizations.

262. Civilization began in the continent of Asia.

    A. True

    B. False   Answer

    C. Cannot tell

263. The colonial era was a disaster for Asia.

    A. True

    B. False   Answer

    C. Cannot tell

264. More of the world's population live in Asia than in any other continent.

    A. True

    B. False   Answer

    C. Cannot tell

265. Post-colonial growth first occurred in Singapore.

    A. True

    B. False   Answer [ ]

    C. Cannot tell

266. The continent of Antarctica is smaller than Asia.

    A. True

    B. False   Answer [ ]

    C. Cannot tell

Passage 5

In tropical rainforests the climate remains hot and damp all the year round. In the artic it is cold all year and high up in mountain ranges the climate is much colder than in nearby low-lying lands. Climate is not the same as weather. The weather can change quickly whereas the climate describes the likely weather conditions over a much longer period of time. The world is divided into five climate zones. Polar is the only zone where it is always cold, tropical where it is hot all year round, temperate where there are warm summers and cold winters, desert where it is dry and cool, and forest where the summers are cool and short. Great climate changes have occurred, an example of which is the last ice age. Mankind can affect climate when, for example, he causes great forest fires that create so much smoke that the sun is obscured for months, cooling a region. More recently man has affected the climate as a result of pollution from industry causing the earth to warm through what is called the greenhouse effect.

267. The passage states that the weather in high mountain ranges is cooler than in nearby low-lying areas.

    A. True

    B. False   Answer [ ]

    C. Cannot tell

268. The passage describes how climate can change.

    A. True

    B. False   Answer [ ]

    C. Cannot tell

269. In a tropical rainforest the climate is the same winter and summer.

    A. True

    B. False   Answer [ ]

    C. Cannot tell

270. In deserts the winter is cooler than the summer.

    A. True

    B. False   Answer

    C. Cannot tell

271. You can infer from the passage that the artic is a polar climate zone.

    A. True

    B. False   Answer

    C. Cannot tell

Passage 6

The theory goes that everything around us is built up of tiny particles called atoms. Some materials are made up of only one type of atom; these are called elements. An example is hydrogen. Others are made up of different sorts of atom bonded together into molecules. These are called compounds. Water, for example, is a compound made up of molecules that contain two hydrogen and one oxygen atom. The force which holds atoms together is called bonds. Atoms are made up of even smaller particles such as neutrons, electrons and protons. Neutrons and protons are made up of even smaller particles. These have been called quarks and gluons. The search is on for the particles that make up quarks.

272. The atom is the smallest particle of matter.

    A. True

    B. False   Answer

    C. Cannot tell

273. All substances are made up of elements.

    A. True

    B. False   Answer

    C. Cannot tell

274. A molecule is a cluster of atoms held together by bonds.

    A. True

    B. False   Answer

    C. Cannot tell

275. Neutrons are made up of quarks and gluons.

    A. True

    B. False   Answer ☐

    C. Cannot tell

276. It can be inferred from the passage that molecules are made up of neutrons, electrons and protons.

    A. True

    B. False   Answer ☐

    C. Cannot tell

Passage 7

Credit card fraud has reached £500 million despite the introduction of new controls. Figures show that losses to fraud rose by 20 per cent last year. Most frauds result from cards intercepted in the post. One hundred thousand cards were posted to customers every day last year. This represents rich pickings for fraudsters. The banks knew the year would be difficult because it was thought that fraudsters would try to commit as many crimes as possible before new controls were introduced. It is hoped that this time next year the effect of the new measures will be known and that the level of fraud will have fallen considerably.

277. Top of the table of types of fraud are those committed with credit cards stolen from people's post.

    A. True

    B. False   Answer ☐

    C. Cannot tell

278. The new measures are sophisticated anti-fraud strategies.

    A. True

    B. False   Answer ☐

    C. Cannot tell

279. The new measures are already in place.

    A. True

    B. False   Answer ☐

    C. Cannot tell

280. Credit card fraud committed as a result of cards intercepted through the post has reached £500 million.

   A. True

   B. False   Answer ☐

   C. Cannot tell

281. The level of losses to overall credit card fraud rose by 20 per cent.

   A. True

   B. False   Answer ☐

   C. Cannot tell

Passage 8

The ambulance service estimates that as many as 500 lives are lost because of the slower emergency response times caused by road humps. Some claim that road humps, or sleeping policemen as they are sometimes called, cost more lives than are saved as a result of the traffic being slowed. Critics of road humps also claim that they cause more pollution as drivers repeatedly slow down and speed up and that they cause more congestion by disrupting the flow of traffic. Residents complain of the noise of cars crossing them and accelerating away from them. Some of these claims run counter to published research which shows that road humps cause average speeds to drop by 10 mph and as a result save lives. Since 1980 and the widespread introduction of road humps, figures show that the level of deaths and serious injury fell by 60 per cent.

282. Delays to the ambulance service and environmental concerns are raised as objections to road humps.

   A. True

   B. False   Answer ☐

   C. Cannot tell

283. It is fair to say that road humps can save lives and injuries but at a price.

   A. True

   B. False   Answer ☐

   C. Cannot tell

284. Drivers find road humps annoying.

   A. True

   B. False   Answer ☐

   C. Cannot tell

285. Critics believe that traffic would flow more smoothly if road humps were removed.

A. True

B. False   Answer

C. Cannot tell

286. The passage states that it is true that the repeated slowing and accelerating of cars over road humps causes more pollution.

A. True

B. False   Answer

C. Cannot tell

Passage 9

People assume that they go to hospital to get well. However, in the past few years this perception has been challenged by the real risk of acquiring a deadly infection while in hospital. As a consequence, public confidence in the heath service has suffered. An antibiotic-resistant strain of bacteria was first identified in the 1950s. It was a staphylococcus common in abscesses and bloodstream infections and it had become resistant to the antibiotic penicillin. Since then the bacteria have become resistant to a second antibiotic and have become established as a source of infection in many nursing homes and hospitals. Today it is believed to cause about 1,000 deaths each year as a result of hospital-acquired infections. Action that can beat this 'superbug' is simple but expensive. It requires very high levels of hygiene and cleanliness and a programme of testing so that infected patients can be isolated and treated.

287. Staphylococcus infections kill around 1,000 people a year.

A. True

B. False   Answer

C. Cannot tell

288. If clean hospitals had been a priority in the 1950s we would not face this threat today.

A. True

B. False   Answer

C. Cannot tell

289. Staphylococcus became established as a source of infection in many nursing homes and hospitals in the 1950s.

   A. True

   B. False   Answer ☐

   C. Cannot tell

290. Staphylococcus has become a 'superbug'.

   A. True

   B. False   Answer ☐

   C. Cannot tell

291. Infections of the bloodstream are more serious than abscesses.

   A. True

   B. False   Answer ☐

   C. Cannot tell

Passage 10

Recent changes to the postal voting system are considered by election officials to significantly increase the risk of electoral fraud. If it were to be widespread such fraud could discredit the whole electoral process. Greatest concerns centre around the very limited time the new system allows electoral administrators to check that requests for postal ballots are genuine. The government are keen to increase the number of people who cast a vote and believe that people should not be denied a vote simply because they do not apply in good time. Fraud is currently rare and there is so far no evidence of postal votes leading to widespread fraud.

292. The government was warned by electoral administrators that the risk of fraud is now much higher.

   A. True

   B. False   Answer ☐

   C. Cannot tell

293. There is currently insufficient fraud to bring the electoral system into disrepute.

   A. True

   B. False   Answer ☐

   C. Cannot tell

294. The previous system of postal voting was considered by election administrators to be less open to fraud.

    A. True

    B. False Answer [   ]

    C. Cannot tell

295. There is a process for checking the validity of applications for postal votes.

    A. True

    B. False Answer [   ]

    C. Cannot tell

296. It is clear that the author of the passage agrees with the concerns raised by the administrators.

    A. True

    B. False Answer [   ]

    C. Cannot tell

Passage 11

Oil prices have been at record levels and are currently at around $45 a barrel. In the most efficient oil fields it costs only 80 to 90 cents to extract a barrel. Most producing countries want greater oil price stability and fear for the effect on their economies and on world demand when, as in recent years, oil prices have fluctuated between $20 and $50 a barrel. In response, some producers are expanding production capacity in order that they can respond more flexibly to demand and rising prices with greater production. Exploration and research into extraction techniques have been commissioned to investigate ways in which production can be expanded. This exploration and research brought unexpected results. Oil analysts have concluded that there is much more oil in the world than current estimates assume and that new techniques make it possible to extract much more of the known reserves economically than previously thought.

297. The record price for crude oil is $50 a barrel.

    A. True

    B. False Answer [   ]

    C. Cannot tell

298. New extraction techniques allow oil to be extracted at a price of between 80 and 90 cents a barrel.

    A. True

    B. False Answer [   ]

    C. Cannot tell

299. It is reasonable to assume that greater capacity at times of high demand will help stabilize prices.

    A. True

    B. False

    C. Cannot tell

    Answer ☐

300. The passage states that the recent exploration has found new reserves.

    A. True

    B. False

    C. Cannot tell

    Answer ☐

301. It would be reasonable to infer from the passage that oil analysts were impressed by the findings of the exploration and research.

    A. True

    B. False

    C. Cannot tell

    Answer ☐

Passage 12

Solicitors, doctors and priests have all traditionally kept in strict confidence information they hold about or are told by their clients. A doctor will not disclose a patient's illness to anyone but the patient or next of kin. Priests have sought to keep secret the content of what they learn in the confessional and solicitors have guarded carefully the confidentiality of the client–lawyer relationship. However, under certain circumstances all these professions make exceptions and will break confidences. A doctor must by law report injuries they believe are the result of gunshots and conditions that represent serious threats to public health. Priests have provided information to the police in relation to child abuse cases and murder. Solicitors are required to report only suspicions they have of money laundering. Journalists also adopt a code of confidentiality to protect their sources. They have a reputation for being a profession far less likely to break their code even when ordered by the courts. In a number of high-profile cases journalists have chosen to go to jail for contempt of court rather than reveal the source of a story.

302. The passage mentions priests, doctors and solicitors as professions with a confidentiality ethic.

    A. True

    B. False

    C. Cannot tell

    Answer ☐

303. Solicitors are obliged to report a client to the authorities if they suspect them of tax evasion.

    A. True

    B. False   Answer ☐

    C. Cannot tell

304. The passage details circumstances where a client's confidentiality might be broken by all the mentioned professions.

    A. True

    B. False   Answer ☐

    C. Cannot tell

305. All professions have a confidentiality code but some are stricter than others.

    A. True

    B. False   Answer ☐

    C. Cannot tell

306. The passage states that a doctor can be prosecuted if he or she does not report a patient who has suffered gunshot wounds.

    A. True

    B. False   Answer ☐

    C. Cannot tell

Passage 13

In the past 12 months benefit fraud has fallen by £½ billion to its lowest level for over a decade. The fall is equivalent to a 25 per cent drop to 1.5 per cent of the total £100 billion benefit bill. This spectacular fall follows permission for the benefit office to access Inland Revenue taxation data. Benefit officers can now immediately check to see if a claimant is working and claiming benefits intended only for those out of work. This new measure has led to over 80,000 people being caught making false claims. A similar initiative has also succeeded in a substantial cut in the level of fraud committed by claimants of housing benefit. Local authorities are responsible for the administration of this allowance which is awarded to the unemployed and low paid to help with housing costs. Until recently local authority staff had been unable to access central government records to check the information provided by claimants. These checks have so far identified 44,000 claimants who have provided false information in order to make claims for allowances for which they are not eligible.

307. By making it possible to share information, over 120,000 cases of fraud have been detected.

   A. True

   B. False

   C. Cannot tell

   Answer ☐

308. Ten years ago the level of benefit fraud was higher.

   A. True

   B. False

   C. Cannot tell

   Answer ☐

309. Only the unemployed should legitimately claim these benefits.

   A. True

   B. False

   C. Cannot tell

   Answer ☐

310. The tone of the passage suggests that these reductions in fraud are a good thing.

   A. True

   B. False

   C. Cannot tell

   Answer ☐

311. A year ago the level of benefit fraud totalled £2 billion.

   A. True

   B. False

   C. Cannot tell

   Answer ☐

Passage 14

In most parts of the developed world many middle class people ask themselves over and over again should they buy or rent a house. If they live in the United States, Spain, Ireland or the UK then in a loud chorus they answer 'buy'. In these countries house prices have almost doubled over the past seven years. Other parts of the developed world have not seen such house price inflation and anyway, is it realistic to assume that prices will always continue to rise?

   Some people argue that paying rent is like throwing money away and it is better to repay a mortgage and build some equity. But what if house prices fall? A really quite minor adjustment would quickly wipe out the equity of many home owners. If house price inflation is something of the past then home ownership becomes less attractive. Renting too has some advantages. In particular, people who rent find it far easier to move for their work.

312. The passage raises the spectre that homeowners may not always be able to rely on capital growth.

   A. True

   B. False   Answer ☐

   C. Cannot tell

313. Most middle class people in the developed world prefer to own their own home.

   A. True

   B. False   Answer ☐

   C. Cannot tell

314. It is reasonable to infer that fewer people will rent if house prices stop going up in value.

   A. True

   B. False   Answer ☐

   C. Cannot tell

315. Spaniards have seen their homes more than double in value.

   A. True

   B. False   Answer ☐

   C. Cannot tell

316. The passage is written from the standpoint that buying may not always be better than renting.

   A. True

   B. False   Answer ☐

   C. Cannot tell

Passage 15

For most of the last two decades of the previous century the economy of the city of Liverpool was mostly stagnant and far behind that of the rest of the UK. But as other cities have become more expensive Liverpool has become a more popular place in which to invest and live. Liverpool's population dropped from 800,000 after the war to less than 500,000 at the turn of the century. The process of depopulation has now reduced to a trickle and for the first time in decades the working population has grown. The level of unemployment, which once stood at 20 per cent, is down to under 5 per cent. Construction of office space is booming and currently being built are conference complexes, a series of department stores and two 50-floor tower blocks. It is not surprising, therefore, that the working population is expected to grow further still. Low living and housing costs have attracted many public sector organizations to relocate to the city. Forty per cent of the workforce of Liverpool work in this sector and it seems that this trend will continue as over half of the new jobs created are public appointments. Subsidy has played a significant part in attracting jobs and investment. Over £4 billion has been spent in the regeneration of the region and the lion's share of this has been committed to the city of Liverpool itself.

317. The city of Liverpool is no longer a net exporter of people.

A. True

B. False   Answer

C. Cannot tell

318. Forty per cent of the new jobs are public appointments.

A. True

B. False   Answer

C. Cannot tell

319. During the 1990s the economy of the region fell far behind that of the rest of the UK.

A. True

B. False   Answer

C. Cannot tell

320. Without the subsidy fewer jobs would have been attracted to the region.

A. True

B. False   Answer

C. Cannot tell

321. Much of Liverpool's recent success is owed to the fact that the costs of living and housing there are less than other cities in the UK.

A. True

B. False   Answer

C. Cannot tell

4

Numerical Reasoning

Psychometric tests of your numeracy skills are by far the most common type. There are few if any tests that do not include a sub-test of these skills and it is crazy to be judged as a great candidate except for the maths! So get down to some serious score-improving practice now. If you are already good at maths then use these questions to build up your speed and attend ready to press home your advantage to the full.

Everyone can master these questions – it is just that some of us have to practise more than others. If you have to pass such a test to realize your career or educational dream and you hate maths then it is time to get down to some serious work and rise to the challenge.

I have known many candidates who have done just this and you can too. I remember one candidate who wanted to be an airline pilot. He had to pass a test for only a few places against many candidates and he was poor at maths. His prospects looked bad but he did it and he is now flying. The secret to his success was his sheer determination and hard work. He used to go for a run every morning and every car he passed he started to add up the numbers of their number plates. Once he had mastered addition he began to multiply the numbers and then divided them. He did this every day for weeks until the day of the test. By this time his command of mental arithmetic was up there with the very best. You don't have to take up running to succeed in this common area of weakness but you do need to let it take over a bit of your life for a while and to really go for it.

In this chapter you will find 344 practice questions. Again, be prepared for different types of question to suddenly appear. Further practice at both an intermediate and advanced level is available in the Kogan Page Testing Series.

Intermediate

How to Pass Numeracy Tests, 2nd edition, Harry Tolley and Ken Thomas
How to Pass Numerical Reasoning Tests, Heidi Smith

Advanced

How to Pass Advance Numeracy Tests, Mike Bryon
Advanced Numeracy Workbook, Mike Bryon

The key operations

Mental arithmetic

It is common for a test to include a section on mental arithmetic. You are required to work the sums in your head without a calculator or doing any working out on paper. These are easy marks for the well-practised candidate. Sharpening your skills is boring, painful even, but everyone can do it. It is simply a matter of practice. Be sure that you attend for a test confident, fast and accurate in these essential operations. Even if the test you face allows you to use a calculator, you should still attend being able to do these calculations in your head. You will save time if you do.

Below are 100 practice questions of your command of multiplication. I have not provided practice for addition and subtraction as you can devise your own questions for these key operations if necessary (you might change the sign of the following sums to make them, for example, addition instead of multiplication). Even if the test that you face does not include questions of this style, they are essential skills and skills that you must command if you are to triumph in any numeracy test.

Work out the following in your head as quickly as possible. Do not stop practising until you are really quick and accurate. Answers are provided on page 229. Explanations are not provided for the first 64 questions.

1. $? \times 5 = 15$ Answer

2. $7 \times ? = 49$ Answer

3. $? \times 4 = 24$ Answer

4. $11 \times 7 = ?$ Answer

5. $4 \times ? = 24$ Answer

6. $6 \times ? = 54$ Answer

7. $3 \times ? = 36$ Answer

8. $12 \times 12 = ?$ Answer

9. $6 \times ? = 48$ Answer

10. $? \times 4 = 16$ Answer

11. $7 \times 12 = ?$ Answer

12. $? \times 7 = 21$ Answer

13. $9 \times ? = 45$ Answer

14. $? \times 8 = 88$ Answer

15. $7 \times ? = 28$ Answer

16. $3 \times 11 = ?$ Answer

17. $9 \times ? = 63$ Answer

18. $4 \times ? = 360$ Answer

19. $11 \times ? = 121$ Answer

20. $? \times 12 = 60$ Answer

21. $? \times 9 = 54$ Answer

22. $7 \times ? = 63$ Answer

23. $9 \times ? = 90$ Answer

24. $? \times 3 = 99$ Answer

25. $8 \times ? = 32$ Answer

26. $12 \times ? = 60$ Answer

27. $? \times 9 = 99$ Answer

28. $3 \times ? = 21$ Answer

29. $6 \times 7 = ?$ Answer

30. $9 \times ? = 81$ Answer

31. $4 \times ? = 100$ Answer

32. $? \times 9 = 99$ Answer

33. $? \times 6 = 48$ Answer

34. $9 \times 12 = ?$ Answer

35. ? × 5 = 55 Answer ☐

36. 4 × ? = 32 Answer ☐

37. 6 × ? = 42 Answer ☐

38. 5 × ? = 100 Answer ☐

39. 9 × ? = 72 Answer ☐

40. ? × 5 = 20 Answer ☐

41. 15 × ? = 90 Answer ☐

42. 11 × ? = 44 Answer ☐

43. ? × 5 = 30 Answer ☐

44. ? × 8 = 64 Answer ☐

45. ? × 12 = 48 Answer ☐

46. 3 × 6 = ? Answer ☐

47. ? × 6 = 66 Answer ☐

48. 4 × ? = 36 Answer ☐

49. ? × 9 = 72 Answer ☐

50. $4 \times 8 = ?$ Answer

51. $7 \times ? = 42$ Answer

52. $? \times 4 = 36$ Answer

53. $8 \times 8 = ?$ Answer

54. $6 \times ? = 66$ Answer

55. $? \times 8 = 56$ Answer

56. $6 \times 5 = ?$ Answer

57. $3 \times ? = 27$ Answer

58. $? \times 12 = 132$ Answer

59. $8 \times 6 = ?$ Answer

60. $? \times 9 = 81$ Answer

61. $4 \times ? = 28$ Answer

62. $6 \times 6 = ?$ Answer

63. $8 \times ? = 96$ Answer

64. $? \times 4 = 12$ Answer

65. List the factors of 18.   Answer [   ]

Tip: Factors are the numbers that divide exactly into a number. For example, the factors of 12 are 1, 2, 3, 4, 6, 12.

66. List the factors of 27.   Answer [   ]

67. List the factors of 11.   Answer [   ]

68. List the factors of 22.   Answer [   ]

69. List the factors of 36.   Answer [   ]

70. How many factors does 20 have?   Answer [   ]

71. How many factors does 56 have?   Answer [   ]

72. How many factors does 19 have?   Answer [   ]

73. List the factors of 60.   Answer [   ]

74. How many factors does 14 have?   Answer [   ]

75. List the factors of 42.   Answer [   ]

76. How many factors does 37 have?   Answer [   ]

77. List the factors of 16.   Answer [   ]

78. How many factors does 48 have?   Answer [   ]

79. List the factors of 24.   Answer

80. How many factors does 32 have?   Answer

81. How many factors does 34 have?   Answer

82. What is the highest common factor of 8 and 20?   Answer

83. How many common factors do 12 and 18 have?   Answer

84. What is the highest common factor of 21 and 49?   Answer

85. How many common factors do 12 and 16 have?   Answer

86. $12.7 \times 100 = ?$ Answer

87. $16.3 \times 10 = ?$ Answer

88. $376 \div 100 = ?$ Answer

89. $90.6 \times 1{,}000$ Answer

90. $2.4 \div 100 = ?$ Answer

91. $96 \div 10 = ?$ Answer

92. $15.02 \div 1{,}000 = ?$ Answer

93. $3.002 \times 1{,}000 = ?$ Answer

94.　$0.07 \div 10 = ?$　　　　　　　　　　Answer ⬚

95.　$0.03 \times 100 = ?$　　　　　　　　　Answer ⬚

96.　Multiply 20 by 920.　　　　　　　　Answer ⬚

97.　Divide 1,200 by 400.　　　　　　　　Answer ⬚

98.　Multiply 3,000 by 70.　　　　　　　Answer ⬚

99.　Divide 48,000 by 60.　　　　　　　　Answer ⬚

100.　Multiply 600 by 300.　　　　　　　Answer ⬚

Percentages

After mental arithmetic and multiplication the next most essential skills demanded by psychometric tests are percentages. Do these questions to revise your ability in these essential operations. Keep practising until you are confident, fast and accurate. Remember not to use a calculator but feel free to use some scrap paper to do some working.

If the answer is recurring then work the sum to only one decimal place.

Changing fractions to decimals

Tip: Divide 100 by the bottom value of the fraction and then multiply the result by the top value.

Worked example: Find ½ as a percentage.　　　Answer ⬚ 50%

Explanation: $100 \div 2 = 50 \times 1 = 50$

101.　Find 1/5 as a percentage.　　　　　Answer ⬚

102. Find 1/4 as a percentage.   Answer [   ]

103. Find 1/9 as a percentage.   Answer [   ]

104. Find 1/12 as a percentage.   Answer [   ]

105. Find 1/8 as a percentage.   Answer [   ]

106. Find 1/16 as a percentage.   Answer [   ]

107. Find 2/3 as a percentage.   Answer [   ]

108. Find 3/5 as a percentage.   Answer [   ]

109. Find 6/16 as a percentage.   Answer [   ]

110. Find 5/8 as a percentage.   Answer [   ]

111. Find 4/6 as a percentage.   Answer [   ]

112. Find 6/8 as a percentage.   Answer [   ]

113. Find 12/15 as a percentage.   Answer [   ]

114. Find 4/20 as a percentage.   Answer [   ]

115. Find 9/24 as a percentage.   Answer [   ]

116. Find 8/20 as a percentage.   Answer [   ]

117. Find 6/32 as a percentage.   Answer [   ]

118. Find 21/28 as a percentage.   Answer [   ]

119. Find 25/80 as a percentage.   Answer [   ]

Changing between decimals and percentages

Tip: Multiply a decimal by 100 to get the equivalent percentage or divide the percentage by 100 to get the equivalent decimal.

Worked example

120. Convert 0.5 into a percentage.   Answer [50%   ]

  Explanation: $0.5 \times 100 = 50$

121. Convert 0.2 to a percentage.   Answer [   ]

122. Convert 0.6 to a percentage.   Answer [   ]

123. Convert 25% to a decimal.   Answer [   ]

124. Convert 0.4 to a percentage.   Answer [   ]

125. Convert 90% to a decimal.   Answer [   ]

126. Convert 0.35 to a percentage.   Answer [   ]

127. Convert 5% to a decimal.   Answer [   ]

128. Convert 0.72 to a percentage.   Answer [   ]

129. Convert 2.4% to a decimal.   Answer [   ]

130. Convert 0.425 to a percentage.   Answer [   ]

131. Convert 1.6% to a percentage.   Answer [   ]

132. Convert 0.333 to a percentage.   Answer [   ]

133. Convert 120% to a decimal.   Answer [   ]

134. Convert 0.5% to a decimal.   Answer [   ]

Expressing values as percentage

Tip: Make the first value a fraction of the second, reduce the fraction to its simplest term and then convert the fraction into a percentage.

Worked example

135. Find 30 as a percentage of 50.   Answer [60%   ]

   Explanation: $30/50 = 3/5, 100 \div 5 = 20 \times 3 = 60$

136. Find 10 as a percentage of 40.   Answer [   ]

137. Find 2 as a percentage of 5.   Answer [   ]

138. Find 3 as a percentage of 27.   Answer [   ]

139. Find 12 as a percentage of 80.   Answer [   ]

140. Find 4 as a percentage of 16.   Answer [   ]

141. Find 12 as a percentage of 40.   Answer [   ]

142. Find 14 as a percentage of 35   Answer [   ]

143. Find 25 as a percentage of 30.   Answer [   ]

144. Find 10 as a percentage of 12.5.   Answer [   ]

145. Find 0.5 as a percentage of 3.   Answer [   ]

146. Find 0.3 as a percentage of 0.9.   Answer [   ]

147. Find 0.2 as a percentage of 80.   Answer [   ]

148. Find 3.3 as a percentage of 3.   Answer [   ]

149. Find 6 as a percentage of 32.   Answer [   ]

Percentages of quantities

Tip: Convert the percentage to a decimal and then multiply by the quantity but take care that you treat all the values equally and express your answer in the appropriate unit.

Worked example

150. Find 12.5% of £80.   Answer [£10]

   Explanation: $12.5 \div 100 = 0.125$, $80 \times 0.125 = 10$.

151. Find 25% of 5 hours.   Answer [   ]

152. Find 25% of 16 metres.   Answer [   ]

153. Find 5% of £5.   Answer

154. Find 20% of 55 metres.   Answer

155. Find 15% of 1 hour 20 minutes.   Answer

156. Find 12% of £360.   Answer

157. Find 12.5% of 3 hours and 40 minutes.   Answer

158. Find 45% of 70 metres.   Answer

159. Find 45% of £20.40.   Answer

160. Find 15% of 3 metres (express your answer in cm).   Answer

161. Find 30% of 24 hours (express your answer in
      hours and minutes).   Answer

162. Find 12% of 250 metres.   Answer

163. Find 17.5% of £1,550.   Answer

164. Find 3% of 72 hours.   Answer

Percentage increase
Tip: Divide the increase by the original amount and multiply the answer by 100.

Worked example

165. What is the percentage increase between 20 and 30?   Answer | 50% |

Explanation: increase = 10, 10 ÷ 20 = 0.5 × 100 = 50

166. What is the percentage increase between 20 and 24?   Answer

167. What is the percentage increase between 40 and 56?   Answer

168. What is the percentage increase between 8 and 9?   Answer

169. What is the percentage increase between 5 and 8?   Answer

170. What is the percentage increase between 16 and 20?   Answer

171. What is the percentage increase between 70 and 91?   Answer

172. What is the percentage increase between 0.5 and 0.7?   Answer

173. What is the percentage increase between 20 and 42?   Answer

174. What is the percentage increase between 5 and 20?   Answer

175. What is the percentage increase between 120 and 124.8?   Answer

176. What is the percentage increase between 36 and 57.6?   Answer

177. What is the percentage increase between 0.1 and 0.35?   Answer [ ]

178. What is the percentage increase between 90 and 97.2?   Answer [ ]

179. What is the percentage increase between 25 and 32.5?   Answer [ ]

Percentage decrease

Tip: Divide the amount of decrease by the original amount and multiply the answer by 100.

Worked example

180. What is the percentage decrease between 100 and 95?   Answer [5%]

Explanation: $100 - 95 = 5$ (the decrease) $5 \div 100 = 0.05 \times 100 = 5$

181. What is the percentage decrease between 40 and 32?   Answer [ ]

182. What is the percentage decrease between 45 and 27?   Answer [ ]

183. What is the percentage decrease between 72 and 36?   Answer [ ]

184. What is the percentage decrease between 120 and 48?   Answer [ ]

185. What is the percentage decrease between 12 and 9?   Answer [ ]

186. What is the percentage decrease between 16 and 4?   Answer [ ]

187. What is the percentage decrease between 70 and 61.6?   Answer [ ]

188. What is the percentage decrease between 56 and 33.6?   Answer [ ]

189. What is the percentage decrease between 220 and 215.6? Answer ☐

190. What is the percentage decrease between 100 and 78? Answer ☐

191. What is the percentage decrease between 7 and 6.65? Answer ☐

192. What is the percentage decrease between 3.5 and 3.08? Answer ☐

193. What is the percentage decrease between 25 and 17.5? Answer ☐

194. What is the percentage decrease between 30 and 26.4? Answer ☐

195. What is the percentage decrease between 65 and 50.7? Answer ☐

Profit and loss as a percentage of the buying or cost price

In this section calculate the profit or loss as a percentage of the buying or cost price. Tip: To find the percentage profit divide the amount of profit by the buying price and multiply the answer by 100. To find the percentage loss divide the loss by the buying price and multiply the answer by 100. Remember to state in your answer whether the answer is a profit or loss.

Worked example (profit)

196. If the buying price of an item is £10 and the selling price £12 then what is the percentage profit?

Answer | 20% profit

Explanation: 12 − 10 = £2 profit, 2 ÷ 10 = 0.2 × 100 = 20

Worked example (loss)

197. What is the percentage loss if the buying price of an item is £10 and the selling price is £9?

Answer | 10% loss

Explanation: 10 − 9 = £1 loss, 1 ÷ 10 = 0.1 × 100 = 10

198. What is the percentage profit or loss if the buying price is £40 and the selling price is 32?

      Answer [   ]

199. What is the percentage profit or loss if the buying price is £50 and the selling price is £70?

      Answer [   ]

200. What is the percentage profit or loss if the buying price is £4 and the selling price is £5?

      Answer [   ]

201. What is the percentage profit or loss if the buying price is £8 and the selling price is £7?

      Answer [   ]

202. What is the percentage profit or loss if the buying price is £290 and the selling price is £237.80?

      Answer [   ]

203. What is the percentage profit or loss if the buying price is £82 and the selling price is £63.14?

      Answer [   ]

204. What is the percentage profit or loss if the buying price is £20 and the selling price is £25?

      Answer [   ]

205. What is the percentage profit or loss if the buying price is £370 and the selling price is £358.90?

      Answer [   ]

206. What is the percentage profit or loss if the buying price is £50 and the selling price is £66?

      Answer [   ]

207. What is the percentage profit or loss if the buying price is £12 and the selling price is £2.40?

Answer [   ]

208. What is the percentage profit or loss if the buying price is £6.50 and the selling price is £6.11?

Answer [   ]

209. What is the percentage profit or loss if the buying price is £100 and the selling price is £132?

Answer [   ]

210. What is the percentage profit or loss if the buying price is £5 and the selling price is £5.75?

Answer [   ]

Sequencing

This was once a very fashionable style of question in tests used by employers but today it is less common in employment-related jobs and more likely to be found in IQ tests.

If you find this style of question a complete enigma then take heart, because practice and taking the time to review the explanations of the answers lead to considerable improvements in your score.

There are only a certain number of principles that these questions are based on and once you have realized most of them you know what to look for and can get these questions right very quickly.

211.

?	17	22	27	32	37

Answer [   ]

212.

42	?	26	18	10	2

Answer [   ]

213.

?	6	36	216	1296	7776

Answer [   ]

| 214. | 20 | 25 | 30 | ? | 40 | 45 | Answer | |

| 215. | 6561 | 2187 | 729 | 243 | 81 | ? | Answer | |

| 216. | ? | 75 | 150 | 300 | 600 | 1,200 | Answer | |

| 217. | 23 | 19 | 15 | ? | 7 | 3 | Answer | |

| 218. | 1 | 3 | 9 | ? | 81 | 243 | Answer | |

| 219. | 435 | ? | 609 | 696 | 783 | 870 | Answer | |

| 220. | 607.5 | 202.5 | ? | 22.5 | 7.5 | 2.5 | Answer | |

| 221. | 7 | 9 | 16 | ? | 41 | 66 | Answer | |

| 222. | 125 | 142 | ? | 176 | 193 | 210 | Answer | |

| 223. | 381 | 355 | 329 | 303 | 277 | ? | Answer | |

| 224. | 250 | ? | 40 | 16 | 6.4 | 2.56 | Answer | |

| 225. | 28 | 42 | 56 | ? | 84 | 98 | Answer | |

| 226. | ? | 2 | 2.5 | 4.5 | 7 | 11.5 | Answer | |

| 227. | 1201 | 1302 | 1403 | ? | 1605 | 1706 | Answer | |

| 228. | 100 | 10 | ? | 0.1 | 0.01 | 0.001 | Answer | |

229.

| 200 | 129 | 58 | ? | –84 | –155 |

Answer [ ]

230.

| 18 | 21 | 39 | ? | 99 |

Answer [ ]

231.

| 25 | 10 | ? | 1.6 | 0.64 | 0.256 |

Answer [ ]

232.

| –12 | –34 | ? | –78 | –100 | –122 |

Answer [ ]

233.

| 0.1 | 0.5 | 2.5 | ? | 62.5 | 312.5 |

Answer [ ]

234.

| 15 | 8 | 23 | ? | 54 | 85 |

Answer [ ]

235.

| 10 | ? | 41 | 17 | 52 | 09 |

Answer [ ]

236.

| 2 | 3 | 6 | ? | 108 | 1944 |

Answer [ ]

237.

| 40 | ? | 90 | 135 | 202.5 |

Answer [ ]

238.

| ? | 1332 | 1665 | 1998 | 2331 | 2664 |

Answer [ ]

239.

| 70 | 11 | 81 | 92 | ? | 265 |

Answer [ ]

240.

| 19 | 81 | 86 | 17 | 41 | ? |

Answer [ ]

241.

| 1 | 3 | ? | 9 | 27 | 243 |

Answer [ ]

242.

| 12 | 2.4 | ? | 0.096 | 0.0192 |

Answer [ ]

243.

| 91 | 12 | 01 | 49 | ? | 8207 |

Answer [ ]

| 244. | 1 | 4 | 9 | 16 | ? | 36 | | Answer | |

| 245. | 2 | 3 | 5 | 7 | 11 | ? | 17 | 19 | Answer | |

| 246. | 80 | 07 | ? | 76 | 07 | 40 | | Answer | |

| 247. | 3:4 | 6:8 | 9:12 | 12:16 | ? | | Answer | |

| 248. | 2 | ? | 8 | 32 | 256 | | Answer | |

| 249. | 0.5 | 3 | 18 | ? | 648 | | Answer | |

| 250. | 14 | 91 | 62 | ? | 6 | | Answer | |

| 251. | 15 | ? | 70 | 18 | 52 | 00 | | Answer | |

| 252. | 24 | 17 | 41 | 58 | ? | | Answer | |

| 253. | 3 | 8 | 24 | ? | 4608 | | Answer | |

| 254. | 2401 | 343 | ? | 7 | 1 | | Answer | |

| 255. | 36 | ? | 64 | 81 | 100 | 121 | | Answer | |

| 256. | ? | 2 | 3 | 4 | 6 | 12 | | Answer | |

| 257. | 104 | ? | 130 | 143 | 156 | | Answer | |

| 258. | 67.24 | 8.2 | 9 | ? | 3.24 | 1.8 | | Answer | |

| 259. | 4 | 8 | 16 | ? | 64 | 128 | Answer | |

| 260. | 11 | 38 | ? | 87 | 136 | 223 | Answer | |

| 261. | 1:2 | 2:4 | 3:6 | ? | 5:10 | Answer | |

| 262. | 1 | ? | 5 | 15 | Answer | |

| 263. | 216 | 343 | 512 | 729 | ? | Answer | |

| 264. | 0.75 | 3 | ? | 48 | 192 | 768 | Answer | |

| 265. | ? | 126 | 140 | 154 | 168 | Answer | |

| 266. | 222 | 426 | ? | 032 | Answer | |

| 267. | 9 | 27 | ? | 243 | 729 | Answer | |

| 268. | 12.5 | 2.5 | 0.5 | ? | 0.02 | Answer | |

| 269. | 7 | 11 | 18 | ? | 47 | 76 | Answer | |

| 270. | 144 | 121 | ? | 81 | 64 | Answer | |

| 271. | 1 | 2 | ? | 14 | Answer | |

| 272. | 2 | 4 | 8 | 32 | ? | Answer | |

| 273. | 16 | 64 | ? | 1024 | Answer | |

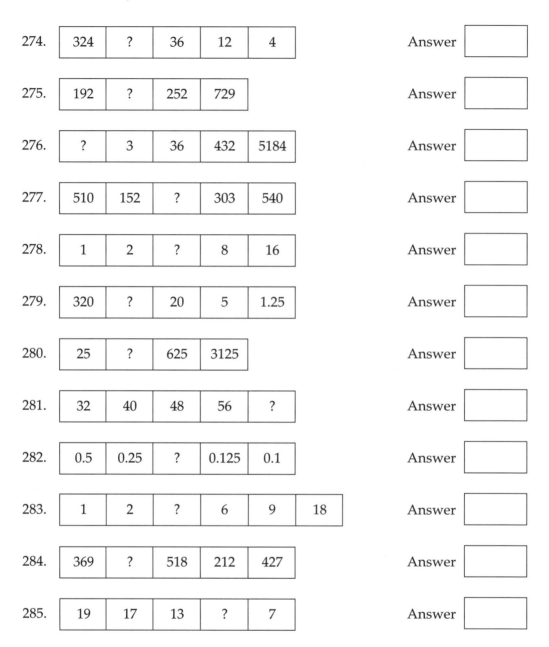

| 274. | 324 | ? | 36 | 12 | 4 | | Answer | |

| 275. | 192 | ? | 252 | 729 | | Answer | |

| 276. | ? | 3 | 36 | 432 | 5184 | Answer | |

| 277. | 510 | 152 | ? | 303 | 540 | Answer | |

| 278. | 1 | 2 | ? | 8 | 16 | Answer | |

| 279. | 320 | ? | 20 | 5 | 1.25 | Answer | |

| 280. | 25 | ? | 625 | 3125 | | Answer | |

| 281. | 32 | 40 | 48 | 56 | ? | Answer | |

| 282. | 0.5 | 0.25 | ? | 0.125 | 0.1 | Answer | |

| 283. | 1 | 2 | ? | 6 | 9 | 18 | Answer | |

| 284. | 369 | ? | 518 | 212 | 427 | Answer | |

| 285. | 19 | 17 | 13 | ? | 7 | Answer | |

Number problems

If you face a psychometric test that comprises this style of question then do not stop practising until you are really quick and get them all right. Others will be doing just that, so you risk coming a poor second unless you do some serious score-improving practice. All the following 59 questions test your command of multiplication and percentages.

More material of this type is available in the Kogan Page titles _How to Pass Selection Tests_ and _How to Pass Graduate Psychometric Tests_. More difficult material is available in _How to Pass Advanced Numeracy Tests_ and _Advanced Numeracy Test Workbook_.

Remember not to use a calculator and instead practise at working the sums manually. You will soon find short cuts and faster methods; some are illustrated in the explanations.

286. If your daily newspaper costs 55p during the week and £1.10 on Saturday and Sunday, how much is your weekly paper bill?

   A. £4.80

   B. £4.85   Answer ☐

   C. £4.90

   D. £4.95

287. If a tub of ice-cream costs £1.20, how much would 6 cost?

   A. £7.00

   B. £7.20   Answer ☐

   C. £7.40

   D. £7.60

288. If a printer produces 30 pages a minute, how many can it print in an hour?

   A. 18

   B. 180   Answer ☐

   C. 1,800

   D. 18,000

289. If forty people donated £6 a month to a charity for one year, how much would be collected?

   A. £288

   B. £2,880   Answer ☐

   C. £28,800

   D. none of these

290. If the utility bill with company A is £18 a month and company B offers the same service for £200 a year, how much if anything can you save a year?

   A. £16

   B. £17   Answer ☐

   C. £18

   D. £19

291. If 200 airline passengers bring 15 kg of hand luggage each, what is the total weight of hand luggage?

    A. 300 kg

    B. 600 kg   Answer ☐

    C. 3,000 kg

    D. 6,000 kg

292. A fabric shop buys 15 metres of material at 75 pence a metre. How much do they pay for the order?

    A. £11.25

    B. £11.50   Answer ☐

    C. £11.75

    D. £12.00

293. If 9 boxes of chocolates weigh 2.7 kg, how much would 4 boxes weigh?

    A. 0.9 kg

    B. 1.2 kg   Answer ☐

    C. 1.5 kg

    D. 1.8 kg

294. If a pump lifts 2,000 litres of water in 8 minutes, how many will it lift in 9 minutes?

    A. 2,500 lt

    B. 2,400 lt   Answer ☐

    C. 2,350 lt

    D. 2,250 lt

295. If you can buy a 300 gm jar of coffee for £7.50 or a 1 kg jar for £26, which purchase represents best value?

    A. 300 gm jar

    B. 1 kg jar   Answer ☐

    C. they are the same

296. If a box holds 8 pairs of shoes and there are a total of 192 shoes to pack away, how many boxes are required?

    A. 8

    B. 10   Answer ☐

    C. 12

    D. 24

297. If a drum holds 40 lt of fuel and there are 15 drums, how much fuel do they contain?

    A. 60 lt

    B. 300 lt   Answer ☐

    C. 600 lt

    D. 900 lt

298. If 50 pencils cost £1.80, how much would 70 cost?

    A. £2.52

    B. £2.53   Answer ☐

    C. £2.54

    D. £2.55

299. If six trays contain 132 eggs, how many does four contain?

    A. 85

    B. 86   Answer ☐

    C. 87

    D. 88

300. If 30 households produce 6,000 bags of rubbish, how many would you expect 5 to produce?

    A. 600

    B. 800   Answer ☐

    C. 1,000

    D. 1,200

301. If your monthly phone bill is always £14 and it includes a quarterly rental of £9.00, how much would you spend in a year on the cost of calls (total cost minus rental)?

   A. £200

   B. £185   Answer [　]

   C. £143

   D. £132

302. If the monthly premium of a life insurance policy cost 70p per £1,000 of insurance cover and a company insures its key staff for a total of £250,000, how much is the cost of the insurance annually?

   A. £2,000

   B. £2,100   Answer [　]

   C. £2,200

   D. £2,300

303. If a worker was paid £5.20 an hour for a 35-hour week and time and a half for any extra hours, how much would he earn if he worked 40 hours?

   A. £218

   B. £219   Answer [　]

   C. £220

   D. £221

304. A computer can be purchased for a deposit of £29 and 18 monthly payments of £16. How much is the total cost of the computer?

   A. £317

   B. £318   Answer [　]

   C. £319

   D. £320

305. If a household uses £1.20 worth of gas every 5 days and the utility company charges 9p standing charge per day, what would you expect the total charge by the utility company for gas to the household to be over a 60-day period?

   A. £19.00

   B. £19.80   Answer [　]

   C. £20.00

   D. £20.80

306. A quality control process results in 30 parts in every 500 being rejected as below standard; express this failure rate as a percentage.

    A. 3%

    B. 6%   Answer ☐

    C. 9%

    D. 12%

307. In his end of year exams Orlando obtained 52 out of 80; express this score as a percentage.

    A. 62%

    B. 63%   Answer ☐

    C. 64%

    D. 65%

308. A survey found that 18 out of 60 respondents preferred dark chocolate to white. What percentage of respondents preferred dark chocolate?

    A. 28%

    B. 29%   Answer ☐

    C. 30%

    D. 31%

309. An employment agency paid its staff £4.32 and charged the client £7.20. What percentage of the charge rate is received by the staff?

    A. 57%

    B. 58%   Answer ☐

    C. 59%

    D. 60%

310. Ella paid £9.68 tax on her earnings of £88; what percentage tax did Ella pay?

    A. 9%

    B. 10%   Answer ☐

    C. 11%

    D. 12%

311. A driver saved £487.50 on his car insurance bill of £650 as a result of his no claims bonus; what percentage discount does this represent?

    A. 60%

    B. 65%   Answer

    C. 70%

    D. 75%

312. A bank charged £120 as an arrangement fee for a personal loan of £4,000; how much did the fee represent as a percentage of the loan?

    A. 3%

    B. 4%   Answer

    C. 5%

    D. 6%

313. A die is thrown 420 times and the number 6 is obtained 63 times; express the frequency of obtaining the number 6 as a percentage.

    A. 13%

    B. 14%   Answer

    C. 15%

    D. 16%

314. A cold-calling advertising campaign results in 126 orders from a total of 6,300 calls; express this rate of success as a percentage.

    A. 0.5%

    B. 1%   Answer

    C. 1.2%

    D. 2%

315. A savings account pays 4% interest; how much would be paid on a deposit of £750?

    A. £29

    B. £30   Answer

    C. £31

    D. £32

316. A train is timetabled to take 3 hours but it is delayed by 15%; how late will the train be?

    A. 25 minutes

    B. 26 minutes   Answer

    C. 27 minutes

    D. 28 minutes

317. A 600 gm box of cereal comes with 12.5% extra; how much extra cereal does the purchaser receive?

    A. 60 gm

    B. 65 gm   Answer

    C. 70 gm

    D. 75 gm

318. A 400-metre length of rope at full stretch becomes 9% longer; how much longer can the rope become?

    A. 36 m

    B. 37 m   Answer

    C. 38 m

    D. 39 m

319. A pump can lift 2,400 litres an hour and its replacement model can lift 2.5% more; how many litres an hour can the new model lift?

    A. 2,440 lt

    B. 2,450 lt   Answer

    C. 2,460 lt

    D. 2,470 lt

320. On the flat a cyclist can average 14 mph but downhill his average speed increases by 40%; what speed does the cyclist average downhill?

    A. 19.5 mph

    B. 19.6 mph   Answer

    C. 19.7 mph

    D. 19.8 mph

321. The minimum payment of a credit card balance is 3%; how much would you have to pay if the card balance stood at £620?

    A. £16.60

    B. £17.60   Answer ▢

    C. £18.60

    D. £19.60

322. On setting A, a motor rotates 3,550 revolutions per minute, and on setting B the motor rotates 20% slower; how many revolutions per minute does the motor make on setting B?

    A. 4,260

    B. 3,850   Answer ▢

    C. 2,840

    D. 710

323. A marathon runner beats her personal best time of 4 hours 30 minutes by 5%; what is her new best time?

    A. 4 hours 16 minutes 30 seconds

    B. 4 hours 17 minutes   Answer ▢

    C. 4 hours 17 minutes and 30 seconds

    D. 4 hours 18 minutes

324. A village population has increased by 3% to 3,605 people; what was the original population?

    A. 3,460

    B. 3,480   Answer ▢

    C. 3,500

    D. 3,510

325. Buying a car with credit is 8% more expensive than the cash price of £7,000; for how much is the car sold if the purchaser is paying with credit?

    A. £7,560

    B. £7,570   Answer ▢

    C. £7,580

    D. £7,590

326. A village population fell over a five-year period by 4% from the original population size of 4,300. How many people now live in the village?

   A. 4,126

   B. 4,128   Answer ☐

   C. 4,130

   D. 4,132

327. The blue party received 8% more votes than the green party's 30,000; how
many votes did the blue party receive?

   A. 32,000

   B. 32,400   Answer ☐

   C. 32,800

   D. 33,200

328. The yellow party received 18% fewer votes than the red party's 22,000; how
many votes did the yellow party obtain?

   A. 17,920

   B. 17,960   Answer ☐

   C. 18,000

   D. 18,040

329. After a discount of 8% a computer is advertised for sale at £552; what was the
price of the computer before the reduction?

   A. £550

   B. £600   Answer ☐

   C. £654

   D. £656

330. When cooled, a length of metal contracts by 2% to a new length of 3 metres;
what was the length of the metal before it was cooled?

   A. 306 cm

   B. 296 cm   Answer ☐

   C. 276 cm

   D. 266 cm

331. Under load a rope stretches 25% and is now 300 metres long; how long was the rope before the load was applied?

   A. 240 m

   B. 230 m   Answer ☐

   C. 220 m

   D. 210 m

332. After an 8% increase Lola's hourly wage is £6.75; what was her hourly wage before the increase?

   A. £6.20

   B. £6.25   Answer ☐

   C. £6.30

   D. £6.35

333. If the value of a car, £6,000, depreciates by 12% a year, how much is it worth after two years?

   A. £4,246.40

   B. £4,446.40   Answer ☐

   C. £4,646.40

   D. £4,846.40

334. If a population increases from 18,000 each year by 5%, what is the population after two years?

   A. 16,245

   B. 17,600   Answer ☐

   C. 18,900

   D. 19,845

335. The time taken to complete an order decreases by 8 seconds to 12 seconds; what is this decrease expressed as an improvement in the efficiency of fulfilling the order?

   A. 16%

   B. 20%   Answer ☐

   C. 40%

   D. 60%

336. If an investment increases from £800 to £1,100, what is the percentage increase?

    A. 37.5%

    B. 39%   Answer

    C. 40.5%

    D. 42%

337. A car was bought for £8,000 and sold for £6,000; what was the percentage loss?

    A. 10%

    B. 15%   Answer

    C. 20%

    D. 25%

338. A watch was bought for £25 and sold for 8% more than the buying price; what was the price it was sold for?

    A. £25

    B. £26   Answer

    C. £27

    D. £28

339. A house was sold for £120,000 at a 4% loss on the purchase price; what was the purchase price?

    A. £115,200

    B. £124,800   Answer

    C. £129,600

    D. £132,800

340. A box of 12 eggs is bought for £1.50 and each egg is sold for 15p; what is the percentage profit?

    A. 20%

    B. 18%   Answer

    C. 15%

    D. 13%

341. Sweets are purchased at £3.00 per kilo and sold for 60p per 100 gm; what is the percentage profit? (Calculate the percentage on the cost or buying price.)

    A. 1,000%

    B. 200%   Answer ☐

    C. 100%

    D. 10%

342. 20 shares were purchased at £2.50 each and sold for a total of £42; what was the percentage profit or loss? (Calculate the percentage on the cost or buying price.)

    A. 13% profit

    B. 14% loss   Answer ☐

    C. 15% profit

    D. 16% loss

343. A company's turnover for a year was £500,000 against total costs of £515,000; what was the percentage loss made by the company that year? (Calculate the percentage on the cost or buying price.)

    A. 0.3%

    B. 1%   Answer ☐

    C. 2%

    D. 3%

344. A Gino Grosso ice-cream machine makes each ice-cream from ingredients that cost only 10p and these are then sold for £1.20 each; what is the percentage profit? (Calculate the percentage on the cost or buying price.)

    A. 110%

    B. 220%   Answer ☐

    C. 660%

    D. 1,100%

5

Personality Questionnaires

Give honest, considered responses to these very common tests but seek to present yourself in the best possible light. Find out about the preferred style of working of the organization and stress those parts of your personality over others. Practise on these questions to make a winning impression.

A personality questionnaire often occurs early in an application process and can serve to reject a great many applicants, so take them seriously. They might be completed online or as a part of the application form. They comprise a number of statements or situations and it is your task to indicate whether you agree or disagree with the sentiment or situation described. They include lots of statements like, for example:

'If colleagues will not listen then it is sometimes necessary to raise your voice.'
'I prefer a working environment where everyone knows their role and responsibilities.'

The test might require you to indicate whether you agree or disagree with the statement, neither agree nor disagree or strongly agree or disagree.

There is not often a right or wrong answer to these questions as your answer will depend on the role and preferred working style of the organization and on your preferences and personality.

Take the first example; most employers would find shouting an inappropriate way to act at work so we should almost certainly disagree with this statement. However, how you answer the second example is completely dependent on your and the organization's preferred way of working and the role in question. Some companies prefer not to work in such a defined way and would prefer not to recruit people who like that style of organization.

Before you answer a personality questionnaire, find out about the organization and decide whether you like its culture and it's the kind of place you will thrive in.

If it is, then apply confident in that knowledge, take time over each question and answer it in a way that shows you as the ideal candidate for the role and company.

It is best not to make too many responses that suggest you neither agree nor disagree as this may be taken to mean that you find it difficult to commit yourself or to make up your mind. Another general point worth remembering is that you should avoid too many agree or disagree strongly responses as this might risk the impression that you have too many strongly held opinions.

The chapter comprises 100 questions typical of those found in real personality questionnaires. They are organized under nine headings typical of key categories of behaviour at work investigated by personality questionnaires. These are:

- your approach to decision making;
- communicating with others;
- your approach to planning;
- managing people and resources;
- motivating yourself and others;
- features of your ideal role;
- your attitude towards risk;
- the secret of your success;
- appropriate responses in work.

Use these practice questions to practise for a real test. Keep at the forefront of your mind the position for which you are looking and the likely culture of the sort of company in the industry of your choice. Many candidates do not take sufficient care or time over the questionnaire and fail to allow themselves enough time to reflect on every question, ensuring that they answer it in a way that supports their application. Always answer the question in the context of how you would act if you were working for the company in the vacant role.

There is no conflict between giving an honest response while presenting yourself in the best possible light. It is perfectly reasonable that you should stress some parts of your personality over others in response to your understanding of the organization's culture and preferred way of working.

Be prepared to make a number of responses that you know will not support your application but to do otherwise would involve making a misleading response. Everyone will answer some questions with low-scoring responses and it is rare for a few to determine the overall result.

Most personality questionnaires do not have a time limit. No answers to most of the practice questions are given, as how you respond will usually depend on your personality and the job and company in question. Explanations are offered of the likely way in which the question may be interpreted.

Your approach to decision making

1. I would not normally expect to be part of the important decision-making process.

    A. Agree strongly

    B. Agree

    C. Do not agree or disagree   Answer ☐

    D. Disagree

    E. Disagree strongly

2. I could make recommendations that went against my personal beliefs.

    A. Agree strongly

    B. Agree

    C. Do not agree or disagree   Answer ☐

    D. Disagree

    E. Disagree strongly

3. Only those qualified in a subject area should contribute to a debate.

    A. Agree strongly

    B. Agree

    C. Do not agree or disagree   Answer ☐

    D. Disagree

    E. Disagree strongly

4. I feel happiest when I can implement defined regulatory processes.

    A. Agree strongly

    B. Agree

    C. Do not agree or disagree   Answer ☐

    D. Disagree

    E. Disagree strongly

5. I expect to take joint responsibility for important decisions and am comfortable to provide a justification for the conclusions reached.

    A. Agree strongly

    B. Agree

    C. Do not agree or disagree   Answer ☐

    D. Disagree

    E. Disagree strongly

6. I would expect most decisions to be based predominantly on numerical information.

    A. Agree strongly

    B. Agree

    C. Do not agree or disagree   Answer ☐

    D. Disagree

    E. Disagree strongly

7. When painful choices have to be made I find it difficult to commit myself.

    A. Agree strongly

    B. Agree

    C. Do not agree or disagree   Answer ☐

    D. Disagree

    E. Disagree strongly

8. When information is incomplete a decision is best deferred.

    A. Agree strongly

    B. Agree

    C. Do not agree or disagree   Answer ☐

    D. Disagree

    E. Disagree strongly

9. The decisions that really shape an organization or policy are best handed down from senior management.

    A. Agree strongly

    B. Agree

    C. Do not agree or disagree   Answer ☐

    D. Disagree

    E. Disagree strongly

10. The views of someone who has been in an organization only a short time are not as valid as those of someone with long service.

    A. Agree strongly

    B. Agree

    C. Do not agree or disagree   Answer ☐

    D. Disagree

    E. Disagree strongly

11. If you know something is right then it is important to keep telling people no matter how repetitive it becomes.

    A. Agree strongly

    B. Agree

    C. Do not agree or disagree   Answer

    D. Disagree

    E. Disagree strongly

12. A compromise is rarely good for business.

    A. Agree strongly

    B. Agree

    C. Do not agree or disagree   Answer

    D. Disagree

    E. Disagree strongly

Communicating with others

13. Above all else my success to date is due to my ability to build and maintain business relationships.

    A. Agree strongly

    B. Agree

    C. Do not agree or disagree   Answer

    D. Disagree

    E. Disagree strongly

14. If a colleague is performing below par then they can expect honest, constructive feedback from me.

    A. Agree strongly

    B. Agree

    C. Do not agree or disagree   Answer

    D. Disagree

    E. Disagree strongly

15. When all the hard work has been done, the key points identified and the recommendations formulated then I feel comfortable if others have the job of selling the policy.

    A. Agree strongly

    B. Agree

    C. Do not agree or disagree   Answer ☐

    D. Disagree

    E. Disagree strongly

16. I pride myself in being able to do a high-pressure job while dealing sensitively with people and issues.

    A. Agree strongly

    B. Agree

    C. Do not agree or disagree   Answer ☐

    D. Disagree

    E. Disagree strongly

17. I have a very direct approach.

    A. Agree strongly

    B. Agree

    C. Do not agree or disagree   Answer ☐

    D. Disagree

    E. Disagree strongly

18. Knowledge is a commodity and so I prefer to keep it to myself.

    A. Agree strongly

    B. Agree

    C. Do not agree or disagree   Answer ☐

    D. Disagree

    E. Disagree strongly

19. I am happiest producing written material and much prefer that role to one that involves presenting an argument orally.

    A. Agree strongly

    B. Agree

    C. Do not agree or disagree   Answer ☐

    D. Disagree

    E. Disagree strongly

20. Being opinionated is not always a bad thing.

    A. Agree strongly

    B. Agree

    C. Do not agree or disagree   Answer

    D. Disagree

    E. Disagree strongly

21. I am used to presenting recommendations to groups of people drawn from all levels of an institution or organization.

    A. Agree strongly

    B. Agree

    C. Do not agree or disagree   Answer

    D. Disagree

    E. Disagree strongly

22. I do not consider it a part of my current job to suggest ways in which something could be done more efficiently.

    A. Agree strongly

    B. Agree

    C. Do not agree or disagree   Answer

    D. Disagree

    E. Disagree strongly

23. Being personable can make up for many potential pitfalls.

    A. Agree strongly

    B. Agree

    C. Do not agree or disagree   Answer

    D. Disagree

    E. Disagree strongly

24. If you can get people to buy into a set of objectives or targets then everyone will work that bit harder towards a shared goal.

    A. Agree strongly

    B. Agree

    C. Do not agree or disagree   Answer

    D. Disagree

    E. Disagree strongly

25. I wish I could more often make novel links between previously unconnected issues.

    A. Agree strongly

    B. Agree

    C. Do not agree or disagree   Answer ☐

    D. Disagree

    E. Disagree strongly

Your approach to planning

26. Always plan for the worst case even if it is very unlikely to happen.

    A. Agree strongly

    B. Agree

    C. Do not agree or disagree   Answer ☐

    D. Disagree

    E. Disagree strongly

27. My greatest attribute is my ability to think strategically while overseeing day-to-day activities.

    A. Agree strongly

    B. Agree

    C. Do not agree or disagree   Answer ☐

    D. Disagree

    E. Disagree strongly

28. You have to take stock, be sure that all the financial needs and objectives are served before you press on with new initiatives.

    A. Agree strongly

    B. Agree

    C. Do not agree or disagree   Answer ☐

    D. Disagree

    E. Disagree strongly

29. Drive and, of course, luck will effect a positive solution to most challenges.

    A. Agree strongly

    B. Agree

    C. Do not agree or disagree   Answer

    D. Disagree

    E. Disagree strongly

30. Accuracy should never be sacrificed to speed.

    A. Agree strongly

    B. Agree

    C. Do not agree or disagree   Answer

    D. Disagree

    E. Disagree strongly

31. Leadership is more about leading people through unforeseen challenges than being able to visualize, communicate and deploy strategies.

    A. Agree strongly

    B. Agree

    C. Do not agree or disagree   Answer

    D. Disagree

    E. Disagree strongly

32. I am 100% customer focused the rest can look after itself.

    A. Agree strongly

    B. Agree

    C. Do not agree or disagree   Answer

    D. Disagree

    E. Disagree strongly

33. Every business can benefit from a few regulations and written procedures but very soon you can have too many and they are bad for business.

    A. Agree strongly

    B. Agree

    C. Do not agree or disagree   Answer

    D. Disagree

    E. Disagree strongly

34. I am entirely comfortable with ambiguity.

    A. Agree strongly
    B. Agree
    C. Do not agree or disagree   Answer ⬜
    D. Disagree
    E. Disagree strongly

35. I excel when faced with a number of competing and demanding tasks but routine administration is something I find demeaning.

    A. Agree strongly
    B. Agree
    C. Do not agree or disagree   Answer ⬜
    D. Disagree
    E. Disagree strongly

36. I like to know what is expected of me and prefer not to have to drop everything to help solve someone else's problems.

    A. Agree strongly
    B. Agree
    C. Do not agree or disagree   Answer ⬜
    D. Disagree
    E. Disagree strongly

37. Delegation is something less committed colleagues do.

    A. Agree strongly
    B. Agree
    C. Do not agree or disagree   Answer ⬜
    D. Disagree
    E. Disagree strongly

Managing people and resources

38. It is better to focus on selling a few more products rather than worry about how much we are spending on stationery.

A. Agree strongly

B. Agree

C. Do not agree or disagree   Answer

D. Disagree

E. Disagree strongly

39. Everyone makes mistakes so it is best if we report them immediately.

A. Agree strongly

B. Agree

C. Do not agree or disagree   Answer

D. Disagree

E. Disagree strongly

40. I would feel uncomfortable in a situation where resources were being used that did not represent best value for money.

A. Agree strongly

B. Agree

C. Do not agree or disagree   Answer

D. Disagree

E. Disagree strongly

41. I understand the importance of effective listening.

A. Agree strongly

B. Agree

C. Do not agree or disagree   Answer

D. Disagree

E. Disagree strongly

42. To manage people well you have to get fully involved in the detail.

   A. Agree strongly

   B. Agree

   C. Do not agree or disagree   Answer

   D. Disagree

   E. Disagree strongly

43. Above all else, good management includes trusting people to do the job.

   A. Agree strongly

   B. Agree

   C. Do not agree or disagree   Answer

   D. Disagree

   E. Disagree strongly

44. Yes, managing people is important but it must come second to fulfilling the client's expectations.

   A. Agree strongly

   B. Agree

   C. Do not agree or disagree   Answer

   D. Disagree

   E. Disagree strongly

45. I wish more credit was given to all the positive outcomes that you can't put numbers on.

   A. Agree strongly

   B. Agree

   C. Do not agree or disagree   Answer

   D. Disagree

   E. Disagree strongly

Motivating yourself and others

46. I may have some faults but a lack of get up and go is not one of them.

    A. Agree strongly

    B. Agree

    C. Do not agree or disagree   Answer

    D. Disagree

    E. Disagree strongly

47. I have always considered myself the best qualified in taking charge of my own personal development.

    A. Agree strongly

    B. Agree

    C. Do not agree or disagree   Answer

    D. Disagree

    E. Disagree strongly

48. In work I prefer to set my own targets and objectives.

    A. Agree strongly

    B. Agree

    C. Do not agree or disagree   Answer

    D. Disagree

    E. Disagree strongly

49. A target is only a target if it is stretching.

    A. Agree strongly

    B. Agree

    C. Do not agree or disagree   Answer

    D. Disagree

    E. Disagree strongly

50. If you want to motivate others successfully, you need to make them feel that they can succeed. Success must be demonstrable and that requires measurable, well-defined performance indicators and feedback.

    A. Agree strongly

    B. Agree

    C. Do not agree or disagree   Answer

    D. Disagree

    E. Disagree strongly

51. Above all else I am motivated by the desire to deliver results.

    A. Agree strongly

    B. Agree

    C. Do not agree or disagree   Answer

    D. Disagree

    E. Disagree strongly

52. I most want a career in which my contribution will make a difference.

    A. Agree strongly

    B. Agree

    C. Do not agree or disagree   Answer

    D. Disagree

    E. Disagree strongly

53. There is no better reward in work than a large salary.

    A. Agree strongly

    B. Agree

    C. Do not agree or disagree   Answer

    D. Disagree

    E. Disagree strongly

54. I am looking for a role without restrictions or barriers.

    A. Agree strongly

    B. Agree

    C. Do not agree or disagree   Answer

    D. Disagree

    E. Disagree strongly

55. It is important for me that I work in a meritocracy.

    A. Agree strongly

    B. Agree

    C. Do not agree or disagree   Answer ☐

    D. Disagree

    E. Disagree strongly

56. I am seeking a role where a different perspective will be valued.

    A. Agree strongly

    B. Agree

    C. Do not agree or disagree   Answer ☐

    D. Disagree

    E. Disagree strongly

Features of your ideal role

Which of the following statements would you like to feature in your next role? What is your approach towards, for example, a demanding role, out of hours working, order or chaos? Employers want to know because they want to recruit someone with the right approach for the vacant role.

Consider the following and decide how you would respond to these questions:

57. I want a job where my cool-headed approach will serve me well.

    A. Agree strongly

    B. Agree

    C. Do not agree or disagree   Answer ☐

    D. Disagree

    E. Disagree strongly

58. I like nothing better than to get my teeth into a challenge.

    A. Agree strongly

    B. Agree

    C. Do not agree or disagree   Answer ☐

    D. Disagree

    E. Disagree strongly

59. I work best when I can get on with my job with the minimum of distractions.

    A. Agree strongly

    B. Agree

    C. Do not agree or disagree   Answer ☐

    D. Disagree

    E. Disagree strongly

60. I feel I perform best in a job where I need to be copied into every e-mail.

    A. Agree strongly

    B. Agree

    C. Do not agree or disagree   Answer ☐

    D. Disagree

    E. Disagree strongly

61. My current job is 24/7 and my next one will be – it goes with the territory.

    A. Agree strongly

    B. Agree

    C. Do not agree or disagree   Answer ☐

    D. Disagree

    E. Disagree strongly

62. I feel resentment if my working life starts to impinge on my home life.

    A. Agree strongly

    B. Agree

    C. Do not agree or disagree   Answer ☐

    D. Disagree

    E. Disagree strongly

63. I prefer a high degree of order and tend to get stressed if things do not go to plan.

    A. Agree strongly

    B. Agree

    C. Do not agree or disagree   Answer ☐

    D. Disagree

    E. Disagree strongly

Your attitude towards risk

An important aspect of an organization's culture and working practice is its approach to risk. Some employers are looking for a safe pair of hands while others want to break from the past and accept that this must involve a degree of risk. Many organizations are governed by procedures and highly regulated and they are looking for people who are comfortable in such a culture.

64. The higher the risk, the higher the potential return.
   A. Agree strongly
   B. Agree
   C. Do not agree or disagree   Answer ☐
   D. Disagree
   E. Disagree strongly

65. The importance of avoiding loss is often underestimated.
   A. Agree strongly
   B. Agree
   C. Do not agree or disagree   Answer ☐
   D. Disagree
   E. Disagree strongly

66. Regulations stifle creativity.
   A. Agree strongly
   B. Agree
   C. Do not agree or disagree   Answer ☐
   D. Disagree
   E. Disagree strongly

67. Success belongs to the bold.
   A. Agree strongly
   B. Agree
   C. Do not agree or disagree   Answer ☐
   D. Disagree
   E. Disagree strongly

68. Provided the customer is happy, everything else should bode well.

    A. Agree strongly

    B. Agree

    C. Do not agree or disagree   Answer ☐

    D. Disagree

    E. Disagree strongly

69. A problem shared is a problem halved.

    A. Agree strongly

    B. Agree

    C. Do not agree or disagree   Answer ☐

    D. Disagree

    E. Disagree strongly

70. It is better to double margins than the customer base.

    A. Agree strongly

    B. Agree

    C. Do not agree or disagree   Answer ☐

    D. Disagree

    E. Disagree strongly

The secret of your success

Choose one of the following with which you agree strongly and is closest to a summary of the secret of your success. Alternatively, choose three with which you disagree. Remember to keep in mind the organizational culture and role for which you are applying.

71. Getting on in business requires ruthlessness.

    A. Agree strongly

    B. Agree

    C. Do not agree or disagree   Answer ☐

    D. Disagree

    E. Disagree strongly

72. I might lack some of the years of experience offered by other candidates but my success comes from the energy and determination that I have to make things happen.

    A. Agree strongly

    B. Agree

    C. Do not agree or disagree   Answer

    D. Disagree

    E. Disagree strongly

73. My success is due to my ability to think strategically while overseeing day-to-day activities.

    A. Agree strongly

    B. Agree

    C. Do not agree or disagree   Answer

    D. Disagree

    E. Disagree strongly

74. Success comes to a great team empowered by exemplary management.

    A. Agree strongly

    B. Agree

    C. Do not agree or disagree   Answer

    D. Disagree

    E. Disagree strongly

75. My success is due to my strong interpersonal skills.

    A. Agree strongly

    B. Agree

    C. Do not agree or disagree   Answer

    D. Disagree

    E. Disagree strongly

76. Drive and determination are the keys to my success.

    A. Agree strongly

    B. Agree

    C. Do not agree or disagree   Answer ☐

    D. Disagree

    E. Disagree strongly

77. My success is due to my ability to think laterally and outside of the box.

    A. Agree strongly

    B. Agree

    C. Do not agree or disagree   Answer ☐

    D. Disagree

    E. Disagree strongly

78. My success is due to my full understanding of the marketplace and competitors' trends.

    A. Agree strongly

    B. Agree

    C. Do not agree or disagree   Answer ☐

    D. Disagree

    E. Disagree strongly

Appropriate responses in work

Employers are increasingly using personality-style tests to try to predict how an applicant, once employed, might conduct themselves in the workplace. In this context the employer is trying to identify the potential employee who might have the wrong approach to, for example: health and safety, equal opportunities, the handling of a grievance or someone in a position of authority.

You need to approach these questions slightly differently. In particular, you must avoid the wrong answers. By this I mean the suggested answers that could imply that you would act inappropriately in work and so should not be employed.

In your current work you may well have a contract of employment and a number of policy documents that form a part of that contract. Read these documents before you complete a personality-style test of this sort as they will help you understand the responsibilities of an employee and what it is reasonable for an employer to expect of you. For example, the grievance procedure should state that you should at the first opportunity inform your manager of any issue that you are feeling unhappy about. The equal opportunities policy will describe how every employee can expect to work in an environment free of the fear of discrimination on the grounds of race, gender or disability and that it is every employee's responsibility to help ensure such an environment. The health and safety policy will require all employees to report immediately anything they consider to represent a danger. These conditions of employment are very similar across all employers.

Use the following questions to decide how you would respond to this style of question in a personality test. Think of the questions from the employer's perspective and ask yourself whether or not a particular suggested answer would present you as a suitable employee.

79. A rude customer cannot expect the same level of service as one who is nice.

A. Agree strongly

B. Agree

C. Do not agree or disagree   Answer

D. Disagree

E. Disagree strongly

80. Sometimes you cannot properly make a point without raising your voice.

A. Agree strongly

B. Agree

C. Do not agree or disagree   Answer

D. Disagree

E. Disagree strongly

81. In work it is sometimes necessary to tell a little lie.

A. Agree strongly

B. Agree

C. Do not agree or disagree   Answer

D. Disagree

E. Disagree strongly

82. If a personal problem arose that affected my performance at work I would inform my line manager straight away.

    A. Agree strongly

    B. Agree

    C. Do not agree or disagree   Answer

    D. Disagree

    E. Disagree strongly

83. There are some types of people you just know you are not going to get on with.

    A. Agree strongly

    B. Agree

    C. Do not agree or disagree   Answer

    D. Disagree

    E. Disagree strongly

84. At work you should avoid upsetting people by telling them something they do not want to hear.

    A. Agree strongly

    B. Agree

    C. Do not agree or disagree   Answer

    D. Disagree

    E. Disagree strongly

85. When something goes wrong it is best to put it right and then report it.

    A. Agree strongly

    B. Agree

    C. Do not agree or disagree   Answer

    D. Disagree

    E. Disagree strongly

86. I prefer to give orders rather than receive them.

    A. Agree strongly

    B. Agree

    C. Do not agree or disagree   Answer

    D. Disagree

    E. Disagree strongly

87. I do not worry too much if a job might be dangerous.

    A. Agree strongly

    B. Agree

    C. Do not agree or disagree   Answer ☐

    D. Disagree

    E. Disagree strongly

88. If someone keeps upsetting me then sooner or later I will get them back.

    A. Agree strongly

    B. Agree

    C. Do not agree or disagree   Answer ☐

    D. Disagree

    E. Disagree strongly

89. If I witnessed someone being bullied I would inform my supervisor.

    A. Agree strongly

    B. Agree

    C. Do not agree or disagree   Answer ☐

    D. Disagree

    E. Disagree strongly

90. A joke at work is normal but some people can't take them and they need to lighten up a bit.

    A. Agree strongly

    B. Agree

    C. Do not agree or disagree   Answer ☐

    D. Disagree

    E. Disagree strongly

91. It's a fact of nature that some jobs women do better than men and others men do better than women.

    A. Agree strongly

    B. Agree

    C. Do not agree or disagree   Answer ☐

    D. Disagree

    E. Disagree strongly

92. Taking a few pens or some paper home from work for the children is something everyone does and it is not really stealing.

    A. Agree strongly
    B. Agree
    C. Do not agree or disagree   Answer ☐
    D. Disagree
    E. Disagree strongly

93. If someone is not pulling their weight then they are being unfair to their colleagues.

    A. Agree strongly
    B. Agree
    C. Do not agree or disagree   Answer ☐
    D. Disagree
    E. Disagree strongly

94. If a customer was angry and unhappy about the service they had received I would listen carefully to their complaint, tell them what I was going to do and report back to them when I had done what I said.

    A. Agree strongly
    B. Agree
    C. Do not agree or disagree   Answer ☐
    D. Disagree
    E. Disagree strongly

95. If I found that I regularly could not complete all my jobs I would stay late to get the job done.

    A. Agree strongly
    B. Agree
    C. Do not agree or disagree   Answer ☐
    D. Disagree
    E. Disagree strongly

96. If I found I could complete all my tasks with time to spare I would offer to help a colleague who was busy.

   A. Agree strongly

   B. Agree

   C. Do not agree or disagree   Answer

   D. Disagree

   E. Disagree strongly

97. I do not think it is right if I am asked to do something that is not in my job description.

   A. Agree strongly

   B. Agree

   C. Do not agree or disagree   Answer

   D. Disagree

   E. Disagree strongly

98. If I choose to have a drink of alcohol at lunch time it is none of my employer's business.

   A. Agree strongly

   B. Agree

   C. Do not agree or disagree   Answer

   D. Disagree

   E. Disagree strongly

99. If I saw something that I considered dangerous I would go out of my way to inform someone in authority.

   A. Agree strongly

   B. Agree

   C. Do not agree or disagree   Answer

   D. Disagree

   E. Disagree strongly

100. I am prepared to argue my corner until I am blue in the face.

    A. Agree strongly

    B. Agree

    C. Do not agree or disagree   Answer ☐

    D. Disagree

    E. Disagree strongly

Non-Verbal Reasoning, Mechanical Comprehension and IQ Tests

If you have been searching for help to prepare for this type of test then you have found it. All you now have to do is settle down somewhere quiet and get practising. Very soon you will be much faster at answering these questions and achieving a much higher score.

There is little practice material generally available for non-verbal and mechanical comprehension tests so this chapter should prove useful to candidates who face these styles of test. I have included practice questions for IQ tests and identified other titles in the Kogan Page Testing Series where further questions of this type can be obtained.

These styles of questions are not as common as they used to be, but you will still come across them, especially to select for courses of study. In these tests, like all sorts of psychometric test, practice can mean the difference between pass and fail. If you face a test that includes this sort of question then set about a programme of practice using questions provided in this chapter.

Non-verbal reasoning

Below are 100 practice questions for non-verbal reasoning tests. Included are three styles of question: identify the feature in common, complete the non-verbal series, and complete the non-verbal matrix, use them to become more confident, fast and accurate. In many tests the questions are based on rotation where a shape is turned, alternation where a shape changes into something else and is then changed back, consistency where a change is made and is then consistently applied, replacement where a shape or shapes are replaced by others, and attention to detail.

The first 30 examples require you to identify from sample shapes the feature they have in common and then select from suggested answer shapes the answer that shares that feature.

The next 50 questions present a series of shapes and you must decide which of the suggested answers is the next step or the missing step in the series.

The last 20 examples involve rows and columns of shapes and it is your task to identify the missing shape from suggested answer shapes.

As with most tests, the examples start easy and get harder. Answers and explanations are provided.

Features in common

1. Identify the suggested answer shapes that share a feature in common with the question shapes.

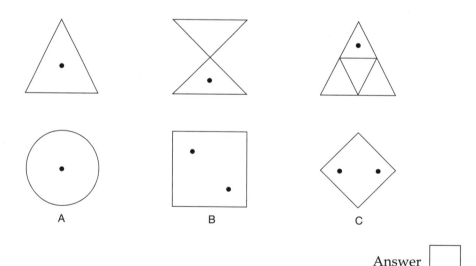

Answer ☐

2. Identify the suggested answer shapes that share a feature in common with the question shapes.

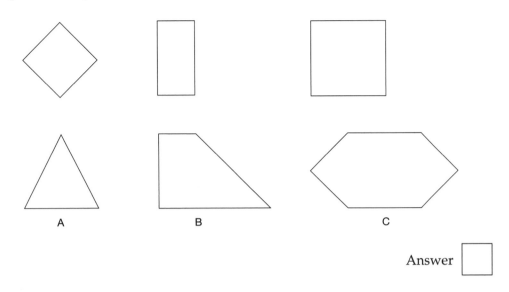

Answer ☐

3. Identify the suggested answer shapes that share a feature in common with the question shapes (the third shape is a triangular-shaped pyramid).

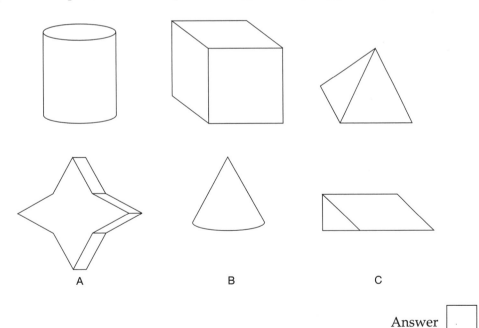

Answer ☐

4. Identify the suggested answer shapes that share a feature in common with the question shapes.

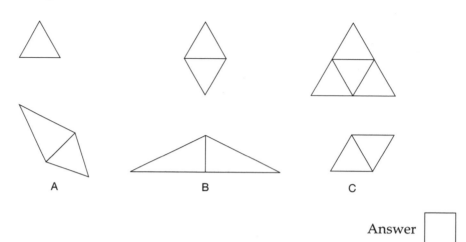

A   B   C

Answer ☐

5. Identify the suggested answer shapes that share a feature in common with the question shapes.

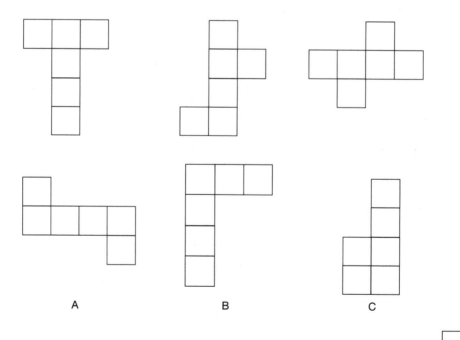

A   B   C

Answer ☐

6. Identify the suggested answer shapes that share a feature in common with the question shapes.

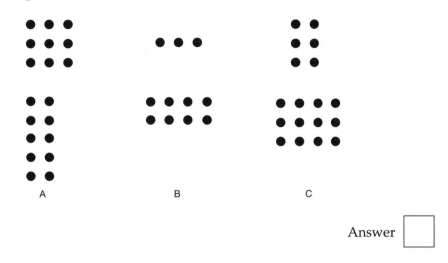

Answer ☐

7. Identify the suggested answer shapes that share a feature in common with the question shapes.

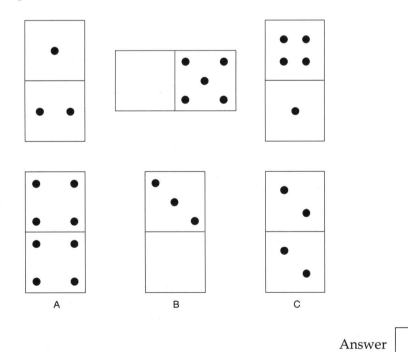

Answer ☐

8. Identify the suggested answer shapes that share a feature in common with the question shapes.

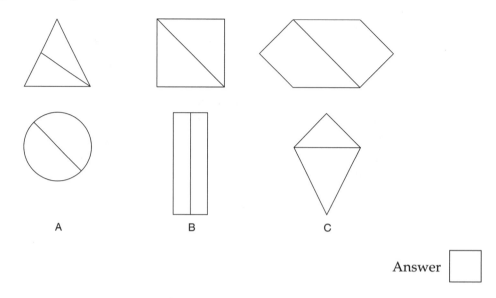

Answer ☐

9. Identify the suggested answer shapes that share a feature in common with the question shapes.

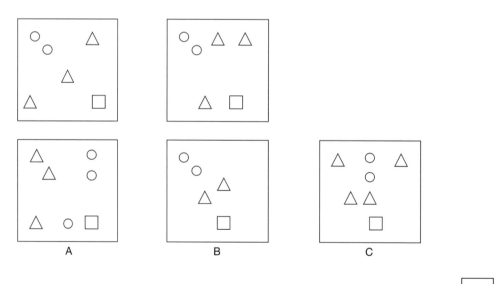

Answer ☐

10. Identify the suggested answer shapes that share a feature in common with the question shapes.

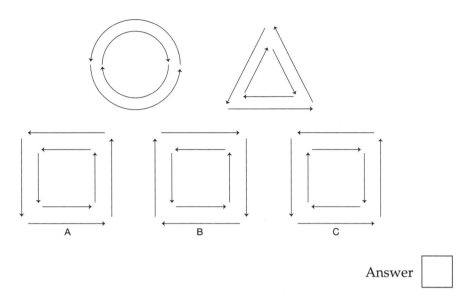

Answer ☐

11. Identify the suggested answer shapes that share a feature in common with the question shapes.

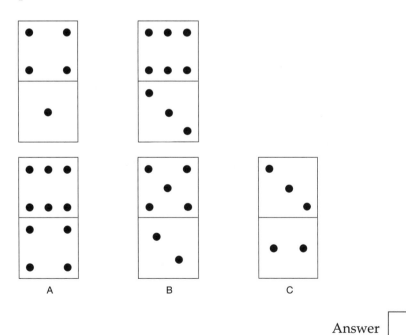

Answer ☐

12. Identify the suggested answer shapes that share a feature in common with the question shapes.

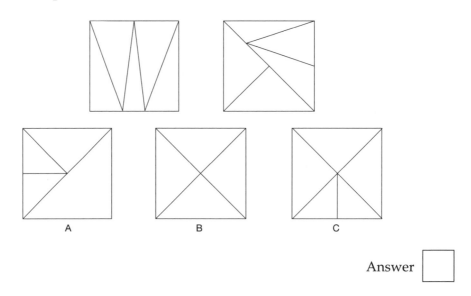

Answer ☐

13. Identify the suggested answer shapes that share a feature in common with the question shapes.

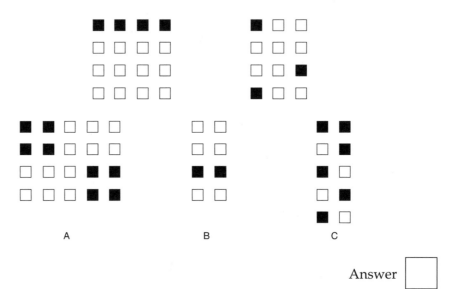

Answer ☐

14. Identify the suggested answer shapes that share a feature in common with the question shapes.

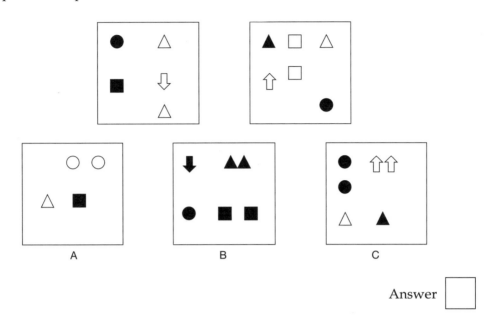

Answer ☐

15. Identify the suggested answer shapes that share a feature in common with the question shapes.

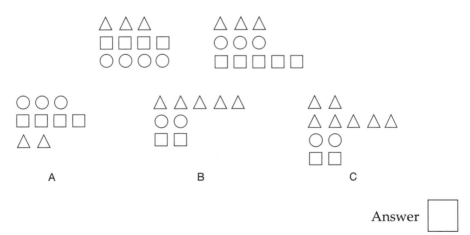

Answer ☐

16. Identify the suggested answer shapes that share a feature in common with the question shapes.

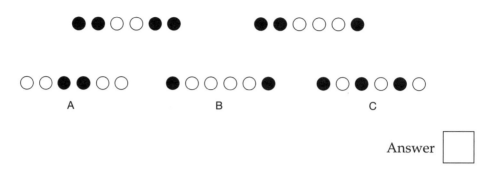

17. Identify the suggested answer shapes that share a feature in common with the question shapes.

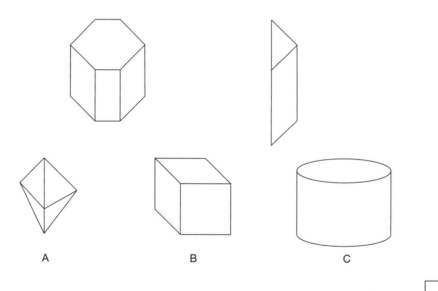

Answer ☐

18. Identify the suggested answer shapes that share a feature in common with the question shapes.

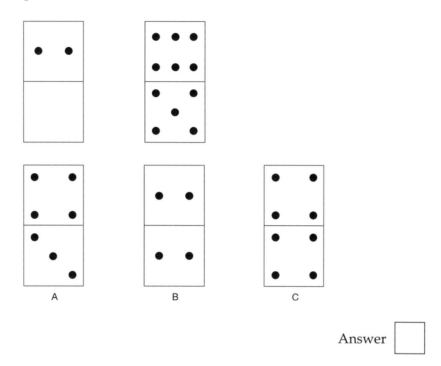

Answer ☐

19. Identify the suggested answer shapes that share a feature in common with the question shapes.

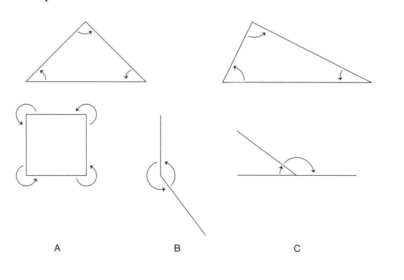

Answer ☐

20. Identify the suggested answer shapes that share a feature in common with the question shapes.

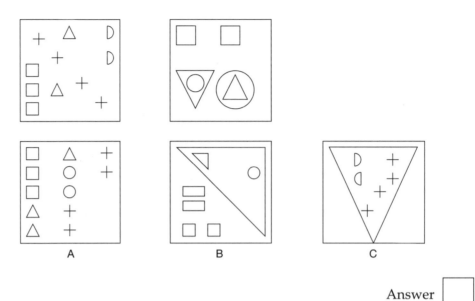

Answer [ ]

21. Identify the suggested answer shapes that share a feature in common with the question shapes.

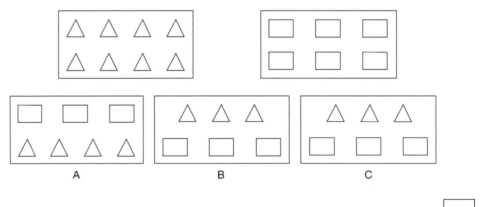

Answer [ ]

22. Identify the suggested answer shapes that share a feature in common with the question shapes.

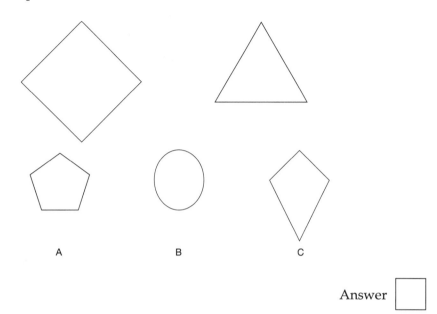

Answer

23. Identify the suggested answer shapes that share a feature in common with the question shapes.

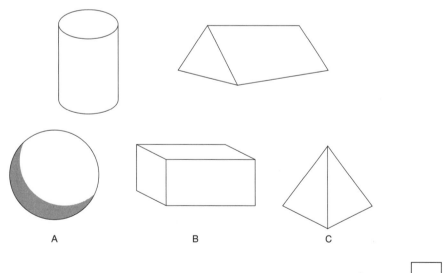

Answer

24. Identify the suggested answer shapes that share a feature in common with the question shapes.

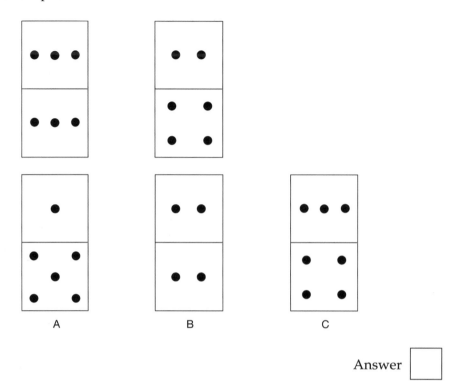

A   B   C

Answer ⬚

25. Identify the suggested answer shapes that share a feature in common with the question shapes.

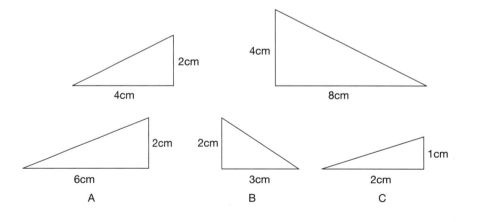

Answer ⬚

26. Identify the suggested answer shapes that share a feature in common with the question shapes.

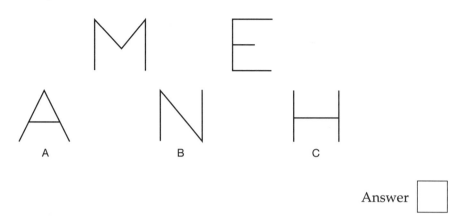

Answer ☐

27. Identify the suggested answer shapes that share a feature in common with the question shapes.

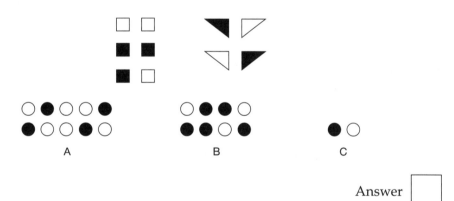

Answer ☐

28. Identify the suggested answer shapes that share a feature in common with the question shapes.

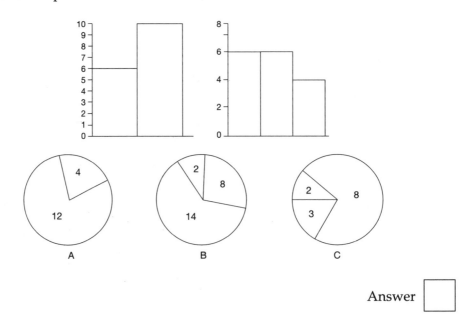

Answer ☐

29. Identify the suggested answer shapes that share a feature in common with the question shapes.

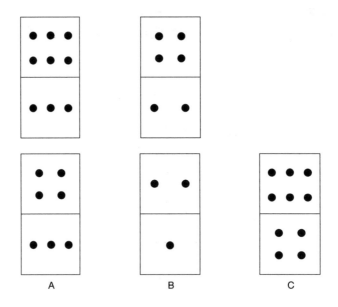

Answer ☐

30. Identify the suggested answer shapes that share a feature in common with the question shapes.

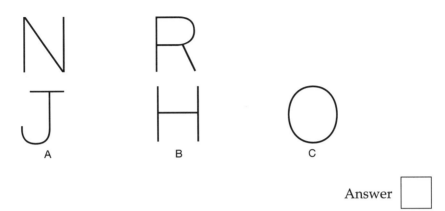

Answer ☐

Find the shape that completes the series

The next 50 questions are non-verbal questions where the shape or shapes form a series. It is your task to identify one of the suggested answers as the missing part of the series or the next step in it.

31. Which of the suggested answers is the next step or the missing step in the series?

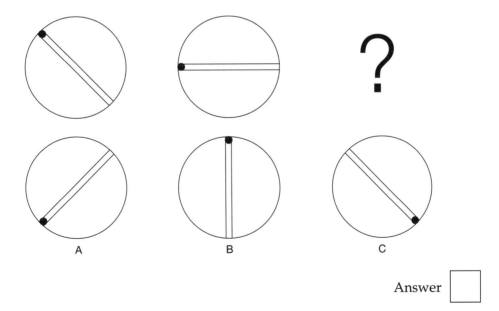

Answer ☐

32. Which of the suggested answers is the next step or the missing step in the series?

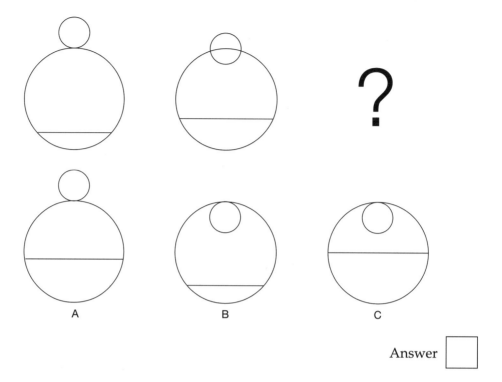

Answer [ ]

33. Which of the suggested answers is the next step or the missing step in the series?

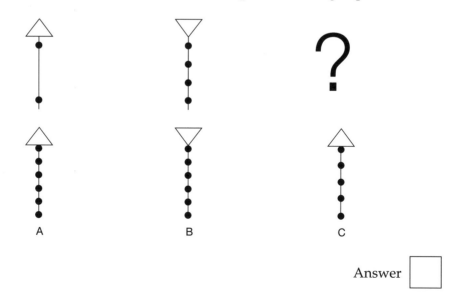

Answer [ ]

34. Which of the suggested answers is the next step or the missing step in the series?

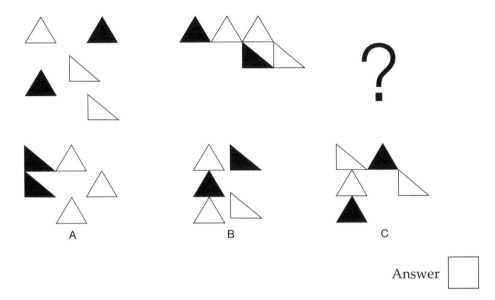

Answer ☐

35. Which of the suggested answers is the next step or the missing step in the series?

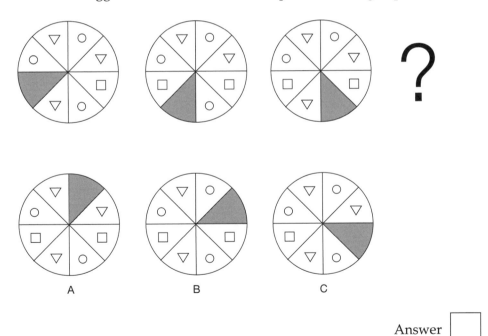

Answer ☐

36. Which of the suggested answers is the next step or the missing step in the series?

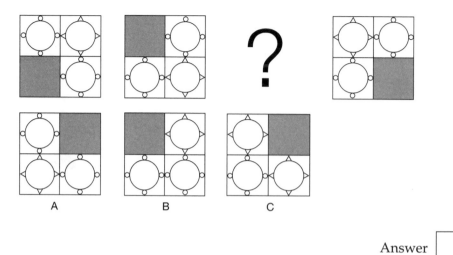

A   B   C

Answer

37. Which of the suggested answers is the next step or the missing step in the series?

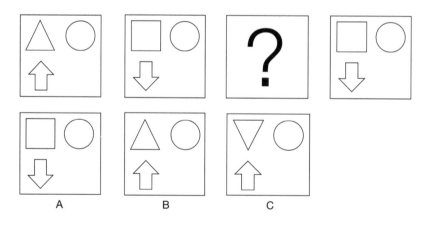

A   B   C

Answer

38. Which of the suggested answers is the next step or the missing step in the series?

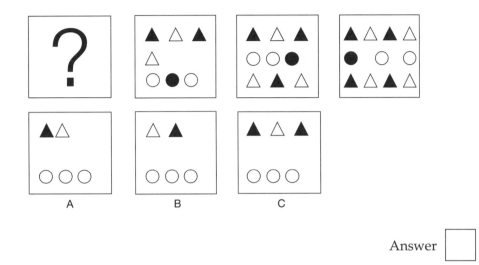

Answer ☐

39. Which of the suggested answers is the next step or the missing step in the series?

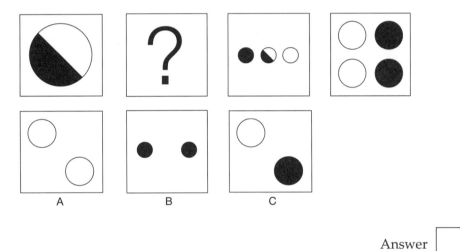

Answer ☐

40. Which of the suggested answers is the next step or the missing step in the series?

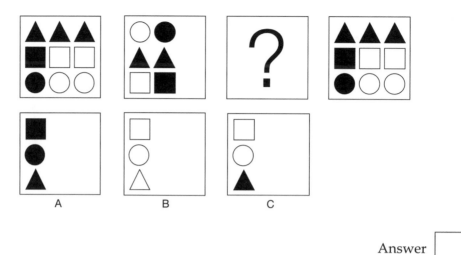

Answer ☐

41. Which of the suggested answers is the next step or the missing step in the series?

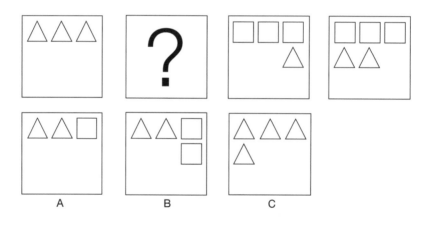

Answer ☐

42. Which of the suggested answers is the next step or the missing step in the series?

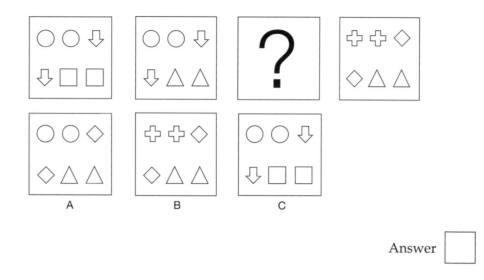

Answer ☐

43. Which of the suggested answers is the next step or the missing step in the series?

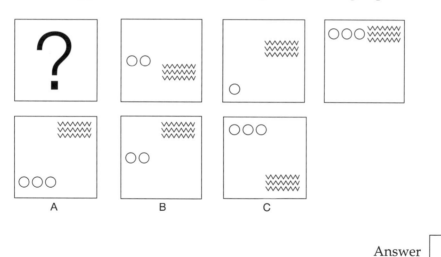

Answer ☐

44. Which of the suggested answers is the next step or the missing step in the series?

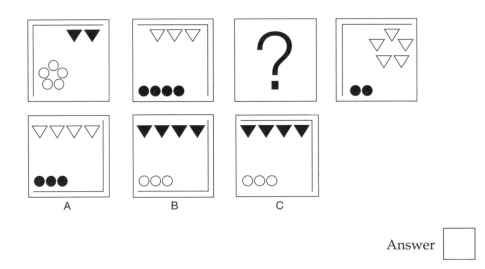

45. Which of the suggested answers is the next step or the missing step in the series?

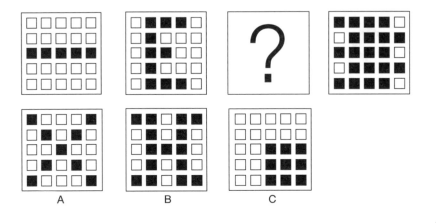

Answer ☐

46. Which of the suggested answers is the next step or the missing step in the series?

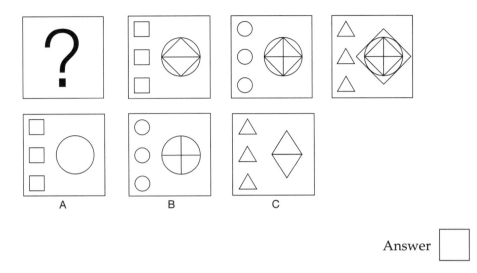

Answer ☐

47. Which of the suggested answers is the next step or the missing step in the series?

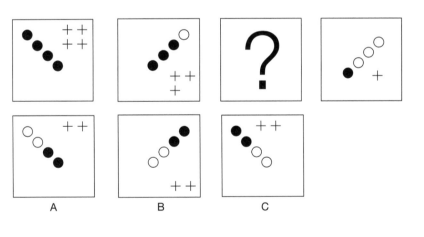

Answer ☐

48. Which of the suggested answers is the next step or the missing step in the series?

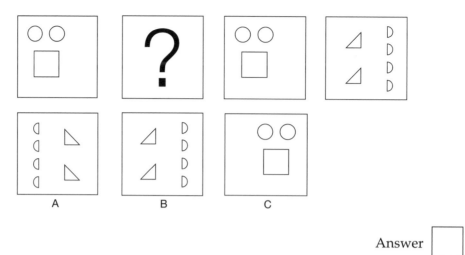

Answer ☐

49. Which of the suggested answers is the next step or the missing step in the series?

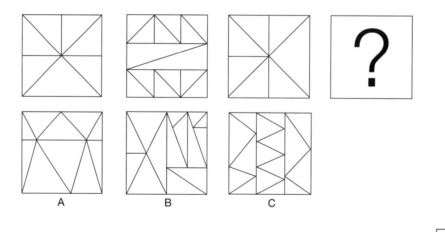

Answer ☐

50. Which of the suggested answers is the next step or the missing step in the series?

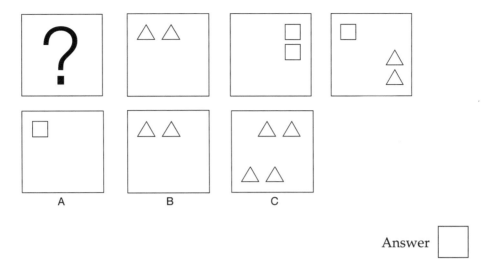

Answer ☐

51. Which of the suggested answers is the next step or the missing step in the series?

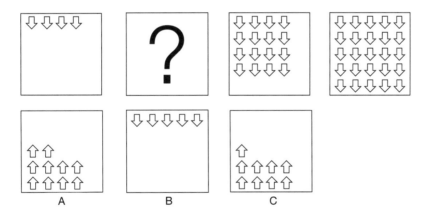

Answer ☐

52.   Which of the suggested answers is the next step or the missing step in the series?

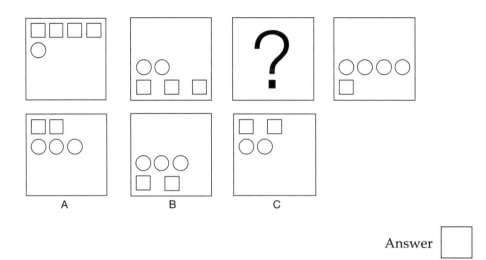

A   B   C

Answer [ ]

53.   Which of the suggested answers is the next step or the missing step in the series?

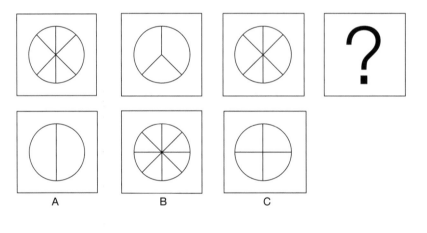

A   B   C

Answer [ ]

54. Which of the suggested answers is the next step or the missing step in the series?

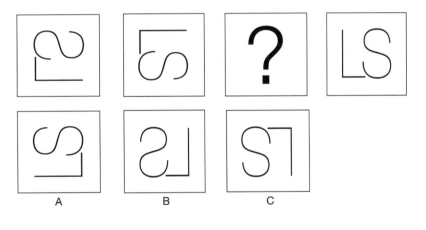

Answer ▢

55. Which of the suggested answers is the next step or the missing step in the series?

Answer ▢

56. Which of the suggested answers is the next step or the missing step in the series?

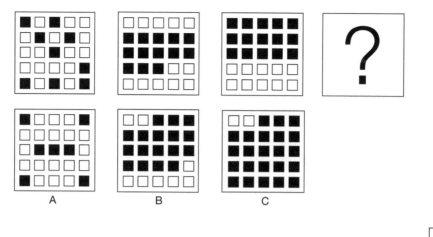

Answer ☐

57. Which of the suggested answers is the next step or the missing step in the series?

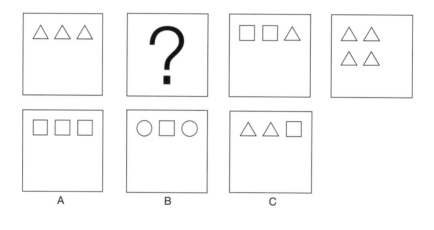

Answer ☐

58. Which of the suggested answers is the next step or the missing step in the series?

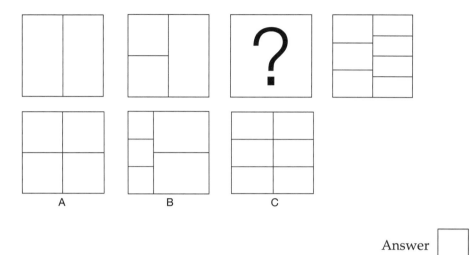

Answer ☐

59. Which of the suggested answers is the next step or the missing step in the series?

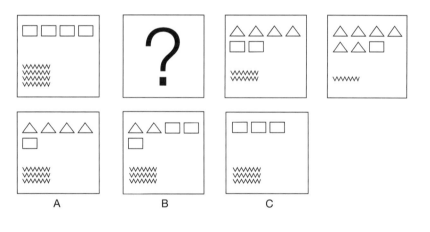

Answer ☐

60. Which of the suggested answers is the next step or the missing step in the series?

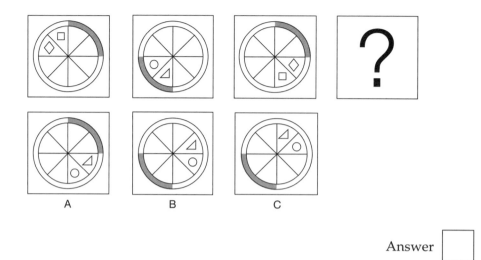

Answer ☐

61. Which of the suggested answers is the next step or the missing step in the series?

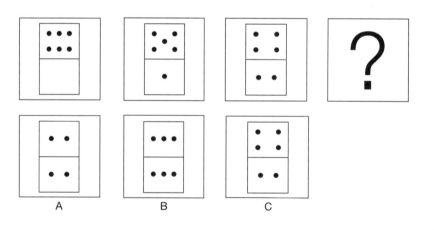

Answer ☐

62. Which of the suggested answers is the next step or the missing step in the series?

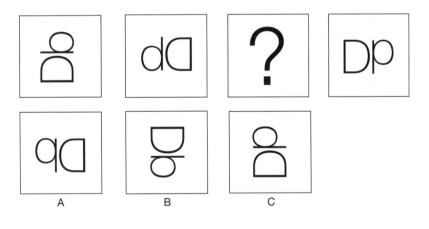

Answer ☐

63. Which of the suggested answers is the next step or the missing step in the series?

Answer ☐

64.   Which of the suggested answers is the next step or the missing step in the series?

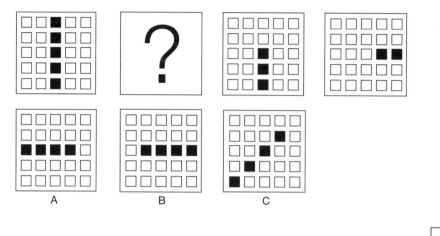

A   B   C

Answer

65.   Which of the suggested answers is the next step or the missing step in the series?

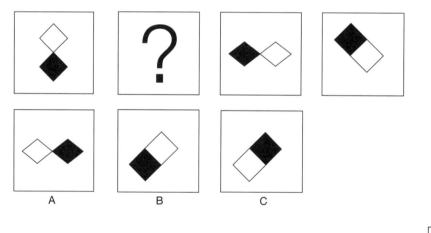

A   B   C

Answer

66. Which of the suggested answers is the next step or the missing step in the series?

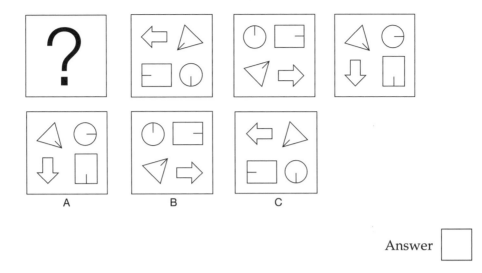

A   B   C

Answer ☐

67. Which of the suggested answers is the next step or the missing step in the series?

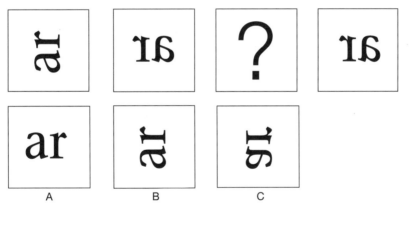

A   B   C

Answer ☐

68. Which of the suggested answers is the next step or the missing step in the series?

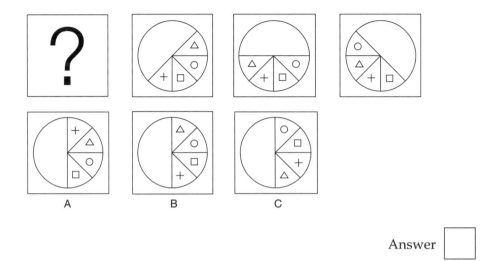

Answer ☐

69. Which of the suggested answers is the next step or the missing step in the series?

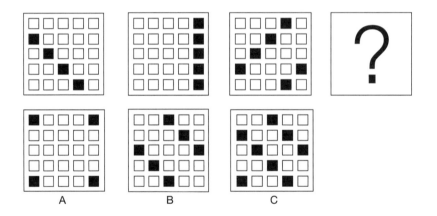

Answer ☐

70. Which of the suggested answers is the next step or the missing step in the series?

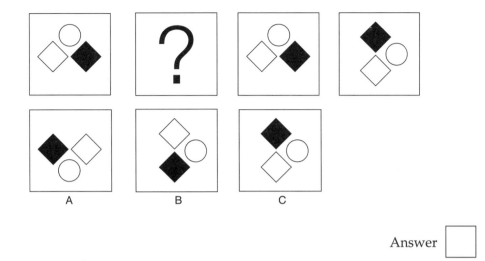

Answer ☐

71. Which of the suggested answers is the next step or the missing step in the series?

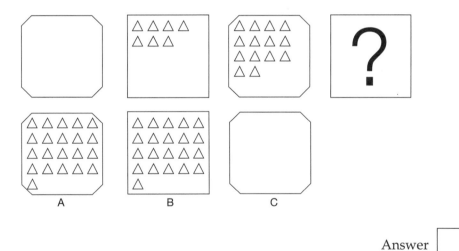

Answer ☐

72. Which of the suggested answers is the next step or the missing step in the series?

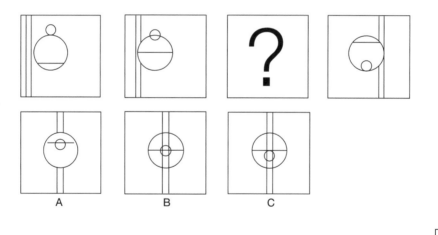

Answer

73. Which of the suggested answers is the next step or the missing step in the series?

Answer

74. Which of the suggested answers is the next step or the missing step in the series?

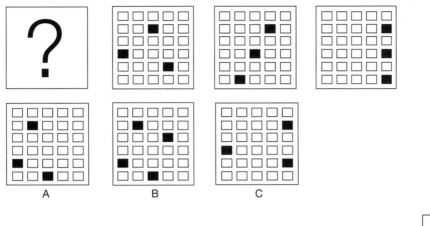

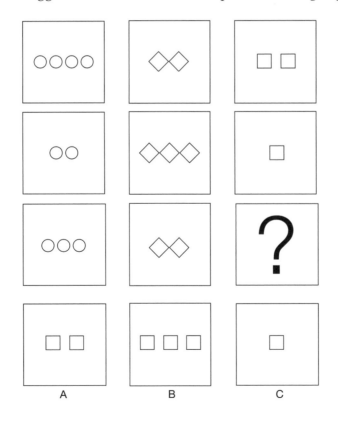

Answer ☐

75. Which of the suggested answers is the next step or the missing step in the series?

Answer ☐

76. Which of the suggested answers is the next step or the missing step in the series?

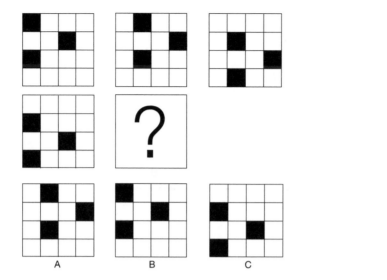

Answer ☐

77. Which of the suggested answers is the next step or the missing step in the series?

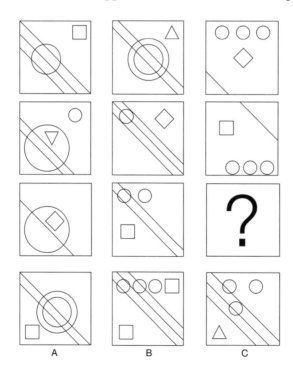

 Answer ☐

78. Which of the suggested answers is the next step or the missing step in the series?

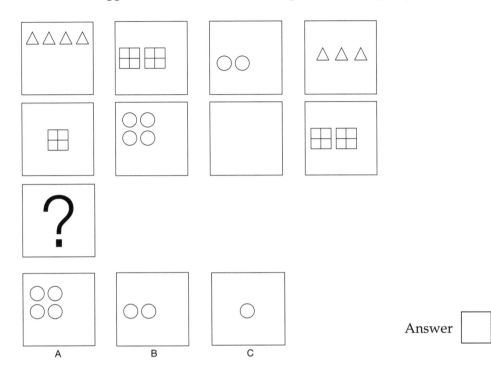

Answer

79. Which of the suggested answers is the next step or the missing step in the series?

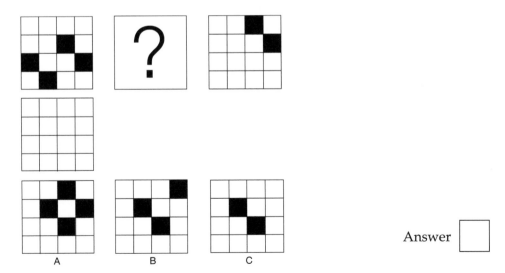

Answer

80.   Which of the suggested answers is the next step or the missing step in the series?

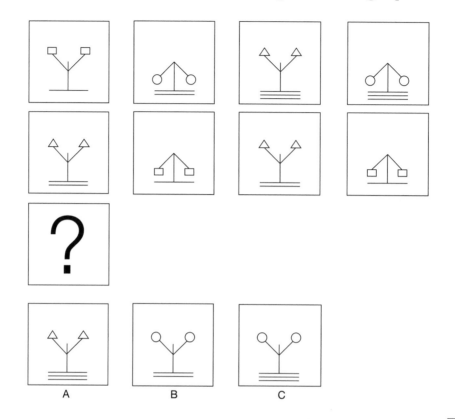

Answer ☐

Completing the series in columns and rows

This style of question requires the series to be continued either horizontally or verti-cally or both. There are 20 examples with answers and explanations.

81.   Identify the suggested answer that correctly completes the series.

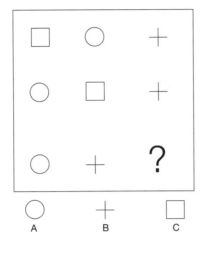

Answer ☐

82.   Identify the suggested answer that correctly completes the series.

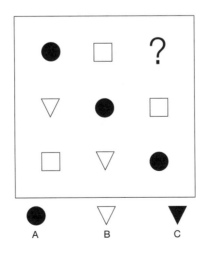

Answer ☐

83. Identify the suggested answer that correctly completes the series.

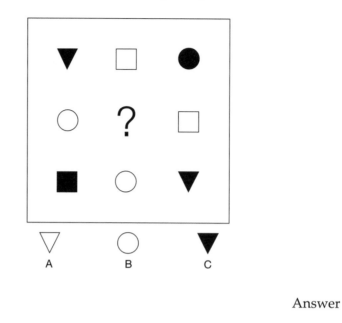

Answer

84. Identify the suggested answer that correctly completes the series.

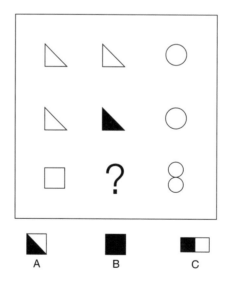

Answer

85. Identify the suggested answer that correctly completes the series.

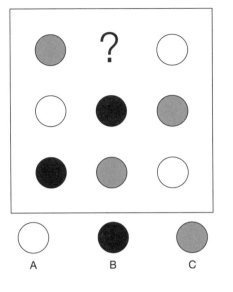

Answer

86. Identify the suggested answer that correctly completes the series.

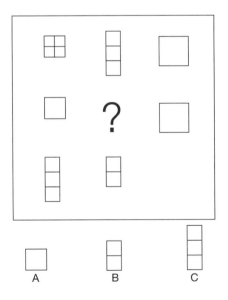

Answer

87. Identify the suggested answer that correctly completes the series.

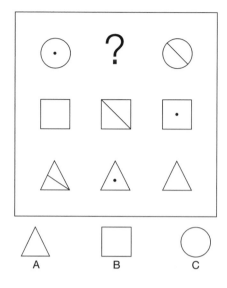

A   B   C

Answer

88. Identify the suggested answer that correctly completes the series.

Answer

89. Identify the suggested answer that correctly completes the series.

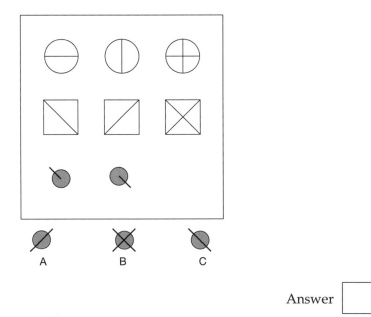

Answer

90. Identify the suggested answer that correctly completes the series.

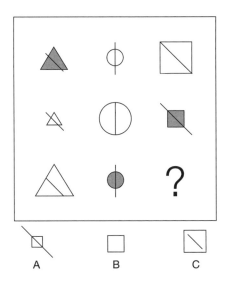

Answer

91. Identify the suggested answer that correctly completes the series.

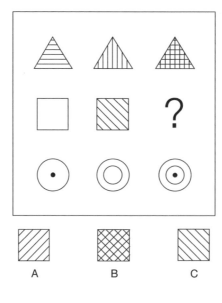

Answer [ ]

92. Identify the suggested answer that correctly completes the series.

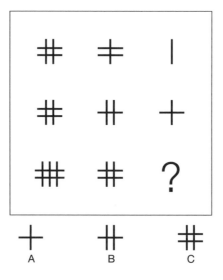

Answer [ ]

93. Identify the suggested answer that correctly completes the series.

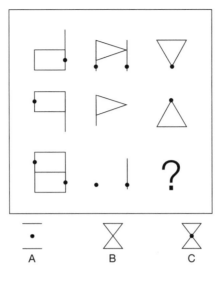

Answer ☐

94. Identify the suggested answer that correctly completes the series.

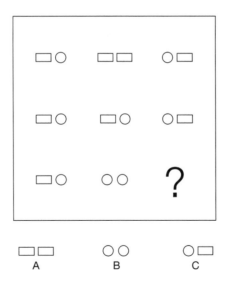

Answer ☐

95. Identify the suggested answer that correctly completes the series.

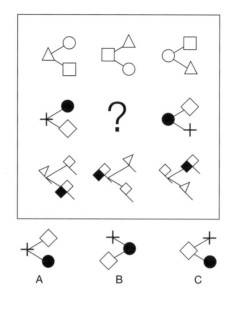

Answer ☐

96. Identify the suggested answer that correctly completes the series.

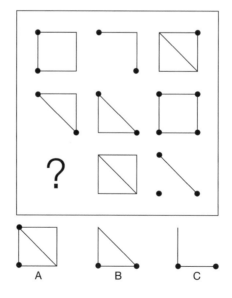

Answer ☐

97. Identify the suggested answer that correctly completes the series.

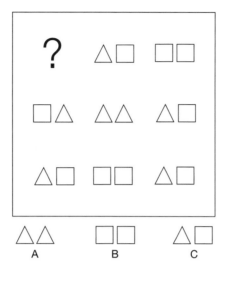

Answer ☐

98. Identify the suggested answer that correctly completes the series.

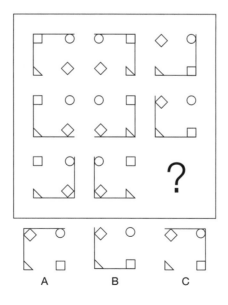

Answer ☐

99. Identify the suggested answer that correctly completes the series.

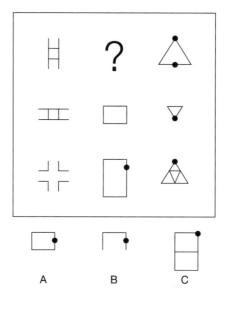

Answer [   ]

100. Identify the suggested answer that correctly completes the series.

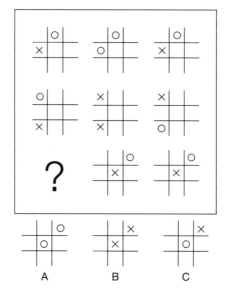

Answer [   ]

Mechanical comprehension

These questions allow you to practise your command of the principles of basic physics and mechanics. Many but not all include a diagram. This style of question is used to select between candidates for positions on apprenticeships and in train-ability tests to select for places on craft courses at colleges.

101.   Which view point would be least prone to error?

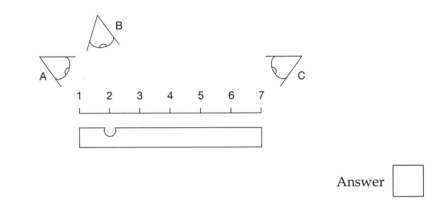

Answer ▢

102.   Which forms of energy does the radio produce?

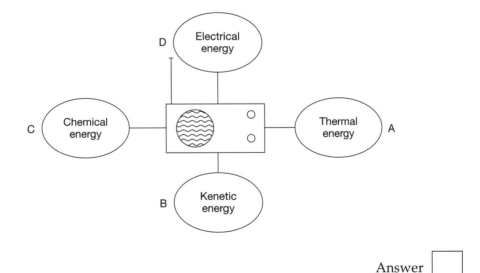

Answer ▢

103. Which transfer of energy occurs when a firework is lit?

Chemical to   A. Elastic

B. Kinetic

C. Thermal   Answer ☐

D. Electromagnetic

E. Gravitational

104. Are the forces between molecules strongest in ice or water?

Answer ☐

105. Which shape has the smallest surface area for a given volume?

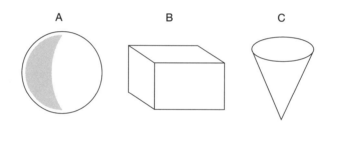

Answer ☐

106. In which clean tube will the water rise the highest?

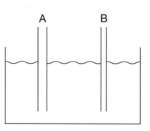

A.

B.

C. The liquid will rise to the same level   Answer ☐

D. The liquid will not rise at all

107 and 108.   Which way does a mercury meniscus curve, if at all?

What is the shape of the meniscus of water?

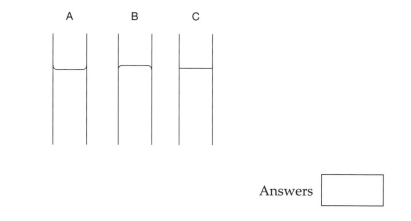

Answers

109.   The split pins A and B hold the iron bar tightly against the blocks C and D; what will happen when the iron bar is heated?

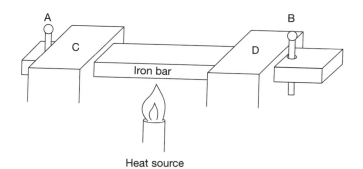

A. The pins will be bent

B. A gap will appear between the pins and the blocks   Answer

C. Nothing

110.   Are these telephone wires drawn as they appear in the summer or winter?

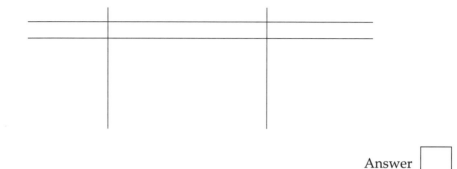

Answer ▢

111.   Which glass beaker is more likely to crack when filled with hot water?

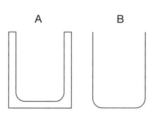

Answer ▢

112.   Which way would the bimetallic strip bend if heat were applied to it or would it stay straight?

A. Bend upwards
B. Bend downwards   Answer ▢
C. Stay straight

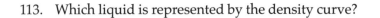

113. Which liquid is represented by the density curve?

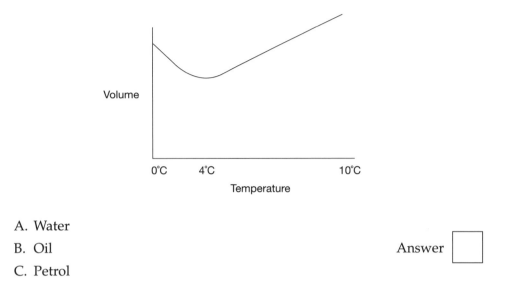

A. Water

B. Oil

C. Petrol

Answer ☐

114. What will happen to the water level in the beaker if the heat source is removed and the air in the glass balloon cools?

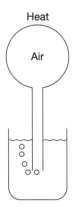

A. Rises

B. Falls

C. Stays the same

Answer ☐

115 and 116.   What will happen when the switch is closed?

What will happen once the bimetallic strip gets hot?

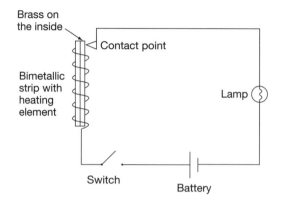

A. The lamp will come on

B. The heating element will warm

C. Both A and B   Answers

D. Neither A nor B

E. Contact will remain once the bimetallic strip gets hot

F. Contact will be broken once the bimetallic strip gets hot

117.   If the temperature remains constant, what will happen to the volume of trapped gas if the pressure is doubled?

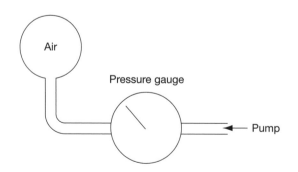

A. The volume it occupies will reduce by a third

B. The volume will double

C. The volume will reduce by a quarter   Answer

D. The volume will reduce by half

118. Which point A on these bars of equal length and thickness would get hottest first?

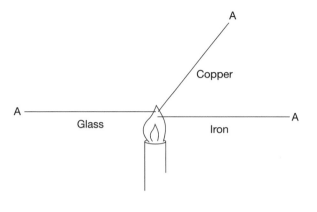

Answer ☐

119. Which liquid would boil last?

A. Water

B. Mercury   Answer ☐

C. Alcohol

120. If a flag was raised on the pole, on which side would it fly?

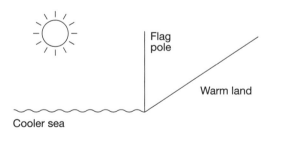

A. The seaside

B. The landside   Answer ☐

C. You cannot tell

121. If left in the sun, in which can will water take longest to warm?

A. Shiny tin can

B. Mat black painted tin can   Answer ☐

122. If a solar panel were located in the northern hemisphere, which way would you expect it to be facing?

A. North

B. South

C. East   Answer ☐

D. West

E. Cannot tell

123. Which way is East?

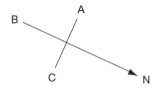

Answer ☐

124. What temperature will the water be?

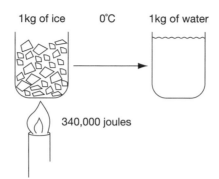

1kg of ice   0°C   1kg of water

340,000 joules

    A. Cannot tell

    B. Warmer than 0°C   Answer

    C. 0°C

125. What will be the temperature of ice made from mineral water?

    A. 0°C

    B. Lower than 0°C   Answer

    C. Higher than 0°C

126. What will happen?

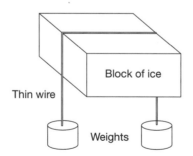

Block of ice

Thin wire

Weights

    A. The block of ice will be cut in half

    B. Nothing   Answer

    C. The wire will eventually drop out of the bottom of the block

127.　What happens when salt is added to boiling water?

　　A. The water will boil more vigorously

　　B. The temperature of the water will fall　　　　Answer ☐

　　C. The water will stop boiling

　　D. The temperature of the water will begin to rise

128.　At what temperature does water boil at altitude?

　　A. 100°C

　　B. Below 100°C　　　　Answer ☐

　　C. Above 100°C

129.　If a package weighed 80 kg in New York, how much would it weigh at the North Pole?

　　A. The same

　　B. Slightly more　　　　Answer ☐

　　C. Slightly less

130.　Which shape is the more rigid?

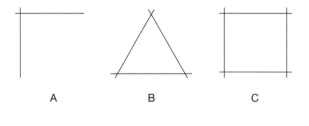

A　　　　　B　　　　　C

Answer ☐

131.　Which is the least and which the most dense?

　　A. Ice

　　B. Water　　　　Answer ☐

　　C. Oil

132. Where is the pressure greatest, at the top, bottom or middle of a drum of water?

Answer [   ]

133. In which direction is the pressure greatest?

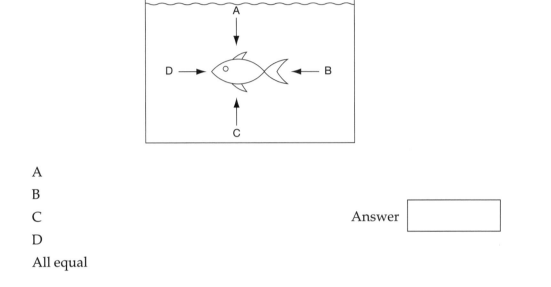

A

B

C   Answer [   ]

D

All equal

134. Which is petrol and which is ice?

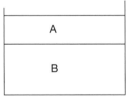

A. Petrol

B. Petrol

A. Ice   Answer [   ]

B. Ice

135. Which barometric reading would you expect on a rainy day?

     A. 970 mbar

     B. 1,010 mbar   Answer

     C. Cannot tell

136. What force holds a nail in a piece of wood?

     A. Molecular expansion

     B. Friction

     C. Molecular bonding   Answer

     D. Conduction

137. Which force cannot act remotely?

     A. Electrical force

     B. Magnetic force

     C. Gravity   Answer

     D. Frictional force

138. When did the vehicle reach a constant speed?

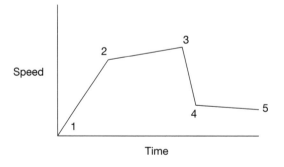

                                               Answer

139. Which shape is in equilibrium?

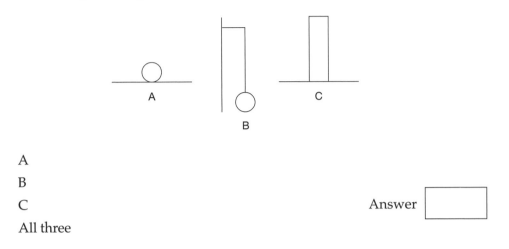

A

B

C   Answer

All three

140. Which line is most likely to represent the centre of gravity of the shape?

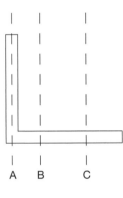

Answer

141. When a gun is discharged the potential energy of the chemical charge is transferred to what?

   A. Actual chemical energy

   B. Electrical energy

   C. Kinetic energy

   D. Elastic energy   Answer

   E. Gravitational energy

   F. Heat and light

142.   Will gear A magnify the force, the distance or both?

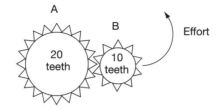

Answer

143.   Which line shows a plane accelerating to take off?

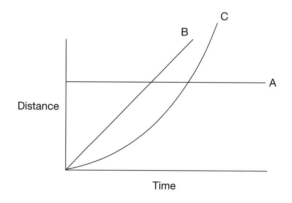

Answer

144. Where is the smaller effort?

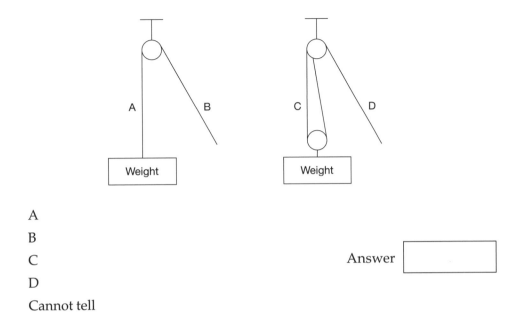

A

B

C

D

Cannot tell

Answer [   ]

145. Which gear is rotating in an anticlockwise direction at 30 revolutions a second?

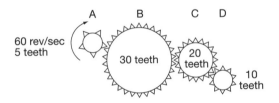

Answer [ ]

146. Is this shape concave or convex?

      A. Concave

      B. Convex

      C. Both   Answer

      D. Neither

147. Which magnets will repel?

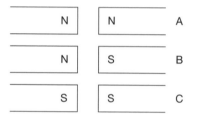

                                         Answer

148. How many colours are there in a rainbow?

      5

      6

      7   Answer

      8

149.   Does A, B or C indicate the correct direction of the electric current?

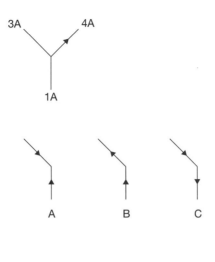

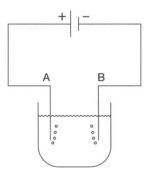

Answer ☐

150.   At which electrode would the most bubbles be produced?

Answer ☐

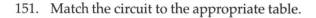

151.   Match the circuit to the appropriate table.

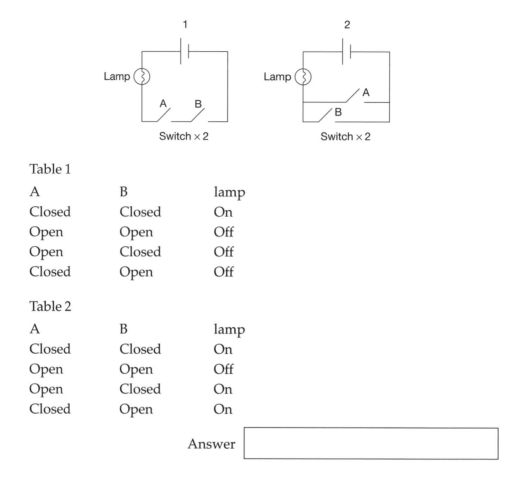

Table 1

A	B	lamp
Closed	Closed	On
Open	Open	Off
Open	Closed	Off
Closed	Open	Off

Table 2

A	B	lamp
Closed	Closed	On
Open	Open	Off
Open	Closed	On
Closed	Open	On

Answer

152.   At what point if any will the rays be stopped?

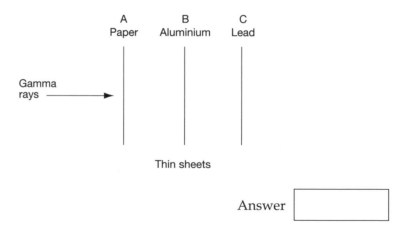

Answer

153. At which point if any will the rays be stopped?

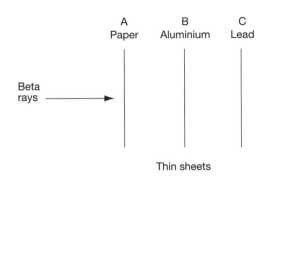

Answer ☐

154. At which point if any will the rays be stopped?

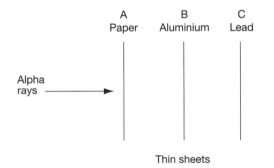

Answer ☐

155. Best complete the energy transfers in this description of a hydroelectric power
      station.

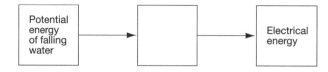

A. Energy in the wires

B. Heat and light

C. Kinetic energy of turbine   Answer

D. Chemical energy

156. If the two identical balls started their descent simultaneously, which would hit
      the ground first?

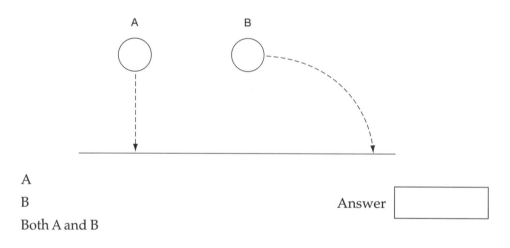

A

B   Answer

Both A and B

157. Which of the tyres is fitted to the vehicle carrying the greatest load?

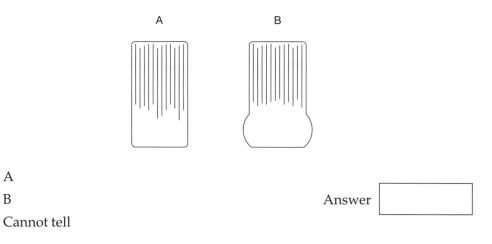

A

B   Answer

Cannot tell

158. If the piston is depressed, at which point is the oil subjected to the greatest pressure?

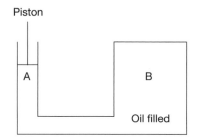

A

B   Answer

All equal

159.   Which seesaw is in equilibrium?

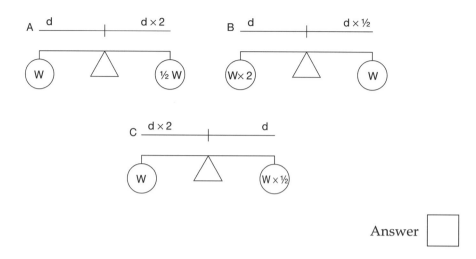

Answer ☐

IQ tests

IQ tests indicate the level of intelligence you were born with and while you can't improve that, you can improve your IQ score. Work through some of these practice questions and then consider the answers and explanations provided in Chapter 7. Return to practise on more of these questions and you will very soon be much faster and accurate at these types of IQ test question. As a result you will get more questions right in a real IQ test and so get a higher IQ score.

You will find hundreds more practice questions in the Kogan Page titles *Test your IQ....*, *Test Your IQ and Psychometric Tests Workbook* by Philip Carter and the CD-Rom *Test your IQ volume 1, The Times Testing Series*.

160.   Find the circle that does not include a word.

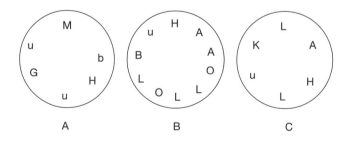

Answer ☐

161. Identify the missing number from the list of suggested answers.

16	?	32
40	48	56

    A. 21

    B. 22

    C. 23   Answer

    D. 24

    E. 25

162. Which is the odd one out?

    A. Felt

    B. Raffia

    C. Velvet   Answer

    D. Chiffon

    E. Oceania

163. Find the missing number from the list of suggested answers.

    16 32 2   8 ? 4

           12 36 3

    A. 30

    B. 31

    C. 32   Answer

    D. 33

    E. 34

164. Find the missing number from the list of suggested answers.

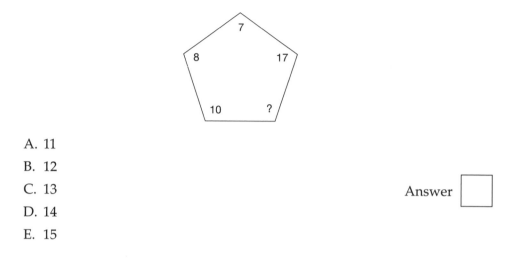

A. 11

B. 12

C. 13   Answer

D. 14

E. 15

165. Find the circle that does not include a word.

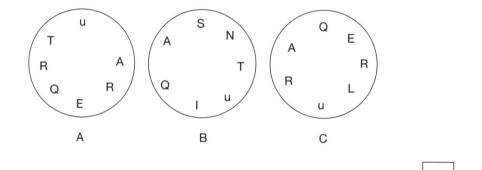

Answer

166. Find the odd one out.

A. Rocking

B. Arm

C. Foot   Answer

D. High

E. Dining

167. Identify the missing number from the list of suggested answers.

66	72	78
84	?	96

A. 88
B. 89
C. 90   Answer
D. 91
E. 92

168. Find the missing number from the list of suggested answers.

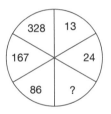

A. 41
B. 42
C. 43   Answer
D. 44
E. 45

169. Identify the word that means the opposite to modern.

Answer

170. Find the odd one out.

    A. India

    B. Cyprus

    C. Austria   Answer ☐

    D. Sudan

    E. Mauritius

171. Identify the missing number from the list of suggested answers.

54	?	72
81	90	99

    A. 60

    B. 61

    C. 62

    D. 63   Answer ☐

    E. 64

    F. 65

172. Find the missing number from the list of suggested answers.

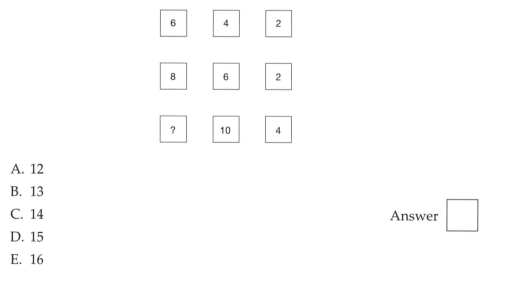

    A. 12

    B. 13

    C. 14   Answer ☐

    D. 15

    E. 16

173. Find the circle that does not include a word.

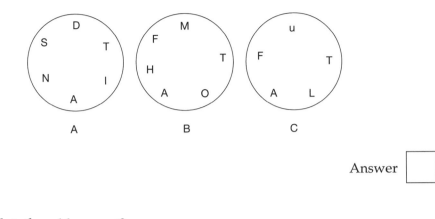

Answer [ ]

174. Which is the odd one out?

A. Humpback

B. Baleen

C. Swing

D. Draw

E. Suspension

Answer [ ]

175. Find the missing number from the list of suggested answers.

A. 3

B. 4

C. 5

D. 6

E. 7

Answer [ ]

176. Find the missing number from the list of suggested answers.

4 20 5   7 21 3

      6 36 ?

A. 3

B. 4

C. 5   Answer

D. 6

177. Find the missing number from the list of suggested answers.

?	63	70
77	84	91

A. 52

B. 53

C. 54   Answer

D. 55

E. 56

178. Which missing letters name an Australian animal?

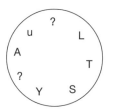

Answer

179. Which is the odd one out?

    A. Cambrian

    B. Scandinavian

    C. Jurassic   Answer ☐

    D. Carboniferous

    E. Triassic

180. Find the box that does not include a word.

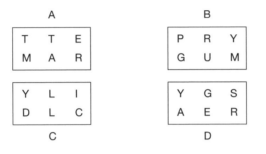

                                                           Answer ☐

181. Find the missing number from the list of suggested answers.

    9 36 4   7 49 ?

           8 48 6

    A. 5

    B. 6

    C. 7   Answer ☐

    D. 8

    E. 9

182. Find the missing number from the list of suggested answers.

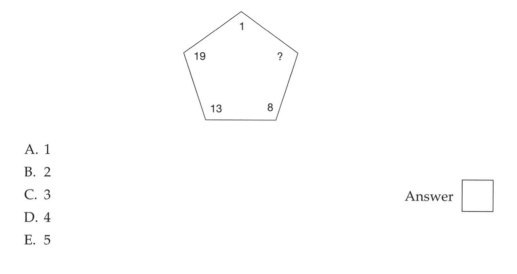

A. 1

B. 2

C. 3   Answer

D. 4

E. 5

183. Which missing letters form a word that is a religion?

Answer

184. Find the missing number from the list of suggested answers.

7 42 6   ? 45 9

6 24 4

A. 3

B. 4

C. 5   Answer

D. 6

E. 7

185. Find the missing number from the suggested answers.

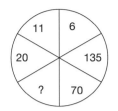

A. 36

B. 37

C. 38   Answer

D. 39

E. 40

186. Which is the odd one out?

A. Fossil

B. Geothermic

C. Chemical   Answer

D. Solar

E. Fission

187. Find the missing number from the suggested list.

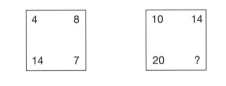

A. 12

B. 13

C. 14   Answer

D. 15

E. 16

188. Find the word that means the same as double.

Answer [   ]

189. Find the odd one out.

    A. Motown

    B. Ragtime

    C. World

    D. Ensemble   Answer [ ]

    E. Gospel

    F. Ambient

190. Find the letters that form the name of a profession.

Answer [   ]

191. Find the missing number from the list of suggested answers.

60	48	?
72	84	96

    A. 33

    B. 34

    C. 35   Answer

    D. 36

    E. 37

192. Which is the odd one out?

    A. Binary

    B. Neutron

    C. Doppler   Answer

    D. Dwarf

    E. Pulsar

193. Find the circle that does not contain a word.

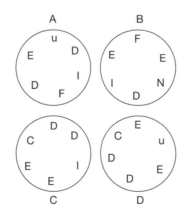

                                     Answer

194. Identify the missing number from the suggested answers.

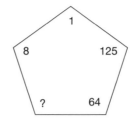

A. 25

B. 26

C. 27   Answer

D. 28

E. 29

195. Which is the odd one out?

A. Christian

B. Baptismal

C. Family   Answer

D. Smith

E. Maiden

F. Stage

196. Find the following shrub.

Answer

197. Which is the odd one out?

    A. Sheet bend

    B. Bowline

    C. Half hitch

    D. Turk's head

    E. Tapir

    F. Monkey's fist

Answer

198. Find the missing number from the suggested answers.

    6 4 5   12 2 7
                ? 3 3

    A. 0

    B. 1

    C. 2

    D. 3

    E. 4

    F. 5

Answer

199. What missing letters make up an edible plant?

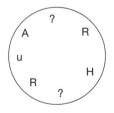

Answer

200.   Which is the odd one out?

A. Green

B. Howler

C. Vervet   Answer [ ]

D. Woolly

E. Capybara

F. Proboscis

201.   Identify the missing number from the suggested answers.

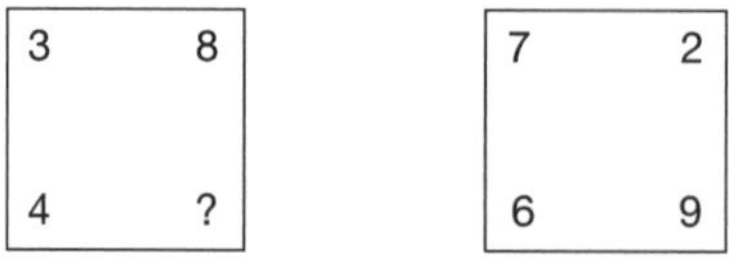

3	8
4	?

7	2
6	9

A. 0

B. 1

C. 2   Answer [ ]

D. 3

E. 4

202.   Which is the odd one out?

A. Mural

B. Fresco

C. Still life   Answer [ ]

D. Cave

E. Pablo

203. Which square contains a word meaning madness?

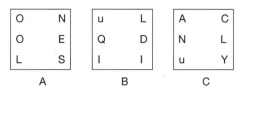

O	N
O	E
L	S

A

u	L
Q	D
I	I

B

A	C
N	L
u	Y

C

Answer ☐

204. Identify the missing number from the suggested answers.

466   835
     26?

A. 5
B. 6
C. 7   Answer ☐
D. 8
E. 9

205. Find the word meaning shocking.

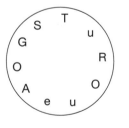

Answer _____

206. Which is the odd one out?

A. Granite

B. Quartz

C. Onyx   Answer ☐

D. Gypsum

E. Mica

F. Calcite

207. Identify the missing number from the suggested answers.

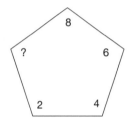

A. 0

B. 1

C. 2

D. 3   Answer ☐

E. 4

F. 5

208. Which is the odd one out?

A. Treble

B. Viola   Answer ☐

C. Cello

D. Cymbals

209. Find a circle that does not contain a word meaning parody.

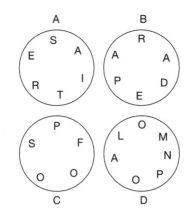

Answer ☐

210. Identify the missing number from the suggested answers.

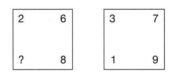

A. 0

B. 1

C. 2   Answer ☐

D. 3

E. 4

211. Which is the odd one out?

A. Pewter

B. Brass

C. Bronze   Answer ☐

D. Tin

E. Silver

212. Find a type of shoe.

Answer

213. Identify the missing number from the suggested answers.

1	4	9
?	25	36

A. 15
B. 16
C. 17   Answer
D. 18

214. Which is the odd one out?
A. Beijing
B. Helsinki
C. Paris   Answer
D. Athens
E. Sydney
F. Wellington

215. Which missing letters make up the name of a seabird?

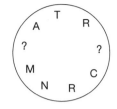

Answer ☐

216. Which is the odd one out?

A. Fable

B. Poem

C. Myth   Answer ☐

D. Legend

E. Saga

217. Identify the missing number from the suggested answers.

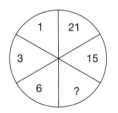

A. 8

B. 9

C. 10   Answer ☐

D. 11

E. 12

218. Which is the odd one out?

   A. Thriller

   B. Western

   C. Romantic   Answer ☐

   D. Legend

   E. Gothic

219. Find the circle that does not contain a word meaning parent.

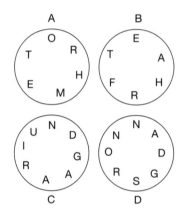

Answer ☐

220. Which is the odd one out?

   A. Penthouse

   B. Terrace

   C. Semi   Answer ☐

   D. Town

   E. Country

221. Identify the missing number from the suggested answers.

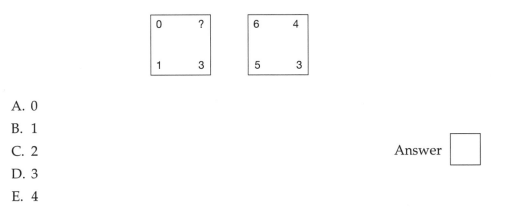

   A. 0
   B. 1
   C. 2   Answer
   D. 3
   E. 4

222. Find the missing letters that make for an unfair election.

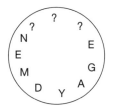

Answer

223. Which is the odd one out?
      A. Ballet
      B. Court   Answer
      C. Deck
      D. Cowboy

224. Identify the missing number from the suggested answers.

036   1 ? 7
            2 5 8

A. 0
B. 1
C. 2   Answer
D. 3
E. 4

225. Which is the odd one out?
A. Isosceles
B. Equilateral
C. Spiral   Answer
D. Right-angle
E. Congruent

226. Find the point north or south of the equator.

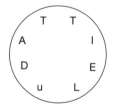

Answer

227. Which is the odd one out?

   A. Sole

   B. Ray

   C. Shearwater   Answer

   D. Tuna

   E. Wrasse

228. Identify the missing number from the suggested answers.

1	2	3
6	?	18

   A. 8

   B. 9

   C. 10   Answer

   D. 11

229. Find the circle that contains a word meaning detail.

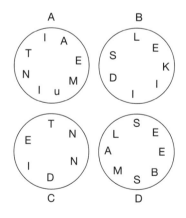

                                                    Answer

230. Which is the odd one out?

    A. Rye

    B. Oats

    C. Millet   Answer ☐

    D. Maize

    E. Marrow

231. Identify the missing number from the suggested answers.

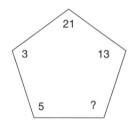

    A. 5

    B. 6

    C. 7

    D. 8   Answer ☐

    E. 9

    F. 10

232. Which is the odd one out?

    A. Cannellini

    B. Sugar

    C. Haricot   Answer ☐

    D. French

    E. Mung

233. Find the word for a diamond.

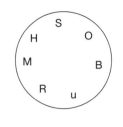

Answer

234. Which is the odd one out?

A. Kite

B. Diamond

C. Plane

D. Rhombus

E. Polygon

F. Square

Answer

7

Answers and Explanations

Verbal reasoning

Word link

1. B Purchase, E Acquisition;   **2.** A Recognition, D Acknowledgement;   **3.** B Liable, F Accountable;   **4.** C Flexible, D Variable;   **5.** C Supplement, D Attachment;   **6.** B Observe, E Respect;   **7.** C Adjoining, F Juxtaposed;   **8.** A Suspension, F Deferral;   **9.** C Arbitrate, D Negotiate;   **10.** A Fix, E Rectify;   **11.** B Counsel, D Advise;   **12.** C Outline, E Sketch;   **13.** B Beneficial, F Favourable;   **14.** C Oppressive, E Wretched;   **15.** C Preceding, D Prior.

Word link – synonyms

16. B aim;   **17.** C affiliate;   **18.** A every;   **19.** C ill-starred;   **20.** A platitudes;   **21.** C imprudent;   **22.** C incidental;   **23.** B outmoded;   **24.** A conclusion;   **25.** C proportion;   **26.** B portray;   **27.** B appraise;   **28.** A primary product, Explanation: A commodity is a raw material or product traded on specialist markets;   **29.** C competitor;   **30.** A agreement, Explanation: Both lease and agreement are types of contract;   **31.** B benefits;   **32.** A utilities;   **33.** C brusque;   **34.** B allocate.

Word link – opposites

35. C Descend;   **36.** A Jovial;   **37.** B Prohibit;   **38.** A Foolish;   **39.** B Rise;   **40.** C Direct;   **41.** C Pacify;   **42.** A Confirm;   **43.** B Despise;   **44.** B Progress;   **45.** D Accelerate;   **46.** B Irresolute;   **47.** C Exhaust;   **48.** C Question;   **49.** A Unprofitable;   **50.** B Lax;   **51.** A Confirm;   **52.** C Crude;   **53.** D Wrong;   **54.** B Work;   **55.** A Deter;   **56.** A agree;   **57.** B sophisticated;   **58.** C beneficial;   **59.** B dawdle;   **60.** A collect;   **61.** B poor;   **62.** C ignore;   **63.** A reality;   **64.** B pleasant;   **65.** A slack;   **66.** C direct;   **67.** B whole;   **68.** C imperceptible;   **69.** B junior;   **70.** C often;   **71.** C incapacitated;   **72.** A optimist;   **73.** B ancestor.

Find the new word(s)

74. tour;   **75.** idle;   **76.** teem;   **77.** only;   **78.** arid;   **79.** gene;   **80.** rely;   **81.** arch;   **82.** tilt (tormentil is a plant);   **83.** urge;   **84.** earl and hove;   **85.** onto;   **86.** rich and chum;   **87.** near;   **88.** dial;   **89.** duty;   **90.** sale;   **91.** seed;   **92.** term;   **93.** note;   **94.** calm;   **95.** chap;   **96.** real;   **97.** tale;   **98.** tear;   **99.** flag;   **100.** cult;   **101.** same;   **102.** meal;   **103.** push;   **104.** only;   **105.** hope;   **106.** bane;   **107.** last;   **108.** must;   **109.** zero;   **110.** race;   **111.** malt;   **112.** ally;   **113.** skin;   **114.** tone;   **115.** deaf;   **116.** palm and opal;   **117.** oust;   **118.** lame and nine;   **119.** etch;   **120.** gasp;   **121.** lush;   **122.** best;   **123.** that and hath;   **124.** sour.

Word swap

125. yourself and someone;   **126.** to and is;   **127.** money and squabbles;   **128.** American and generation;   **129.** result and work;   **130.** as and steady;   **131.** city and café;   **132.** a and each;   **133.** a and the;   **134.** from and on;   **135.** challenging and successful;   **136.** employees and leaders;   **137.** developed and diverse;   **138.** organization and organization's;   **139.** inflation and expansion;   **140.** supplied and powered;   **141.** human and unfashionable;   **142.** bar and suit;   **143.** bull and financial;   **144.** inflation and growth;   **145.** treaty and change;   **146.** 57,000 and 150,000;   **147.** route and signs;   **148.** and and out;   **149.** America and Mexico;   **150.** China and India;   **151.** Manufacturing and outsourcing.

Sentence sequencing

152. C, A, B;   **153.** B, A, C;   **154.** C, A, B;   **155.** C, D, B, A;   **156.** B, C, A, D;   **157.** D, B, A, C;   **158.** B, C, D, A;   **159.** A, C, D, B;   **160.** C, B, D, A;   **161.** C, A, B, D;   **162.** C, A, D, B;   **163.** B, F, D, A, E, C;   **164.** B, A, D, C;   **165.** C, A, B, D;   **166.** B, D, A, C;   **167.** D, C, B, A;   **168.** D, C, B, A;   **169.** D, B, A, C;   **170.** D, B, C, A;   **171.** C, B, A, D;   **172.** B, C, D, A;   **173.** A, C, B;   **174.** B, C, D, A;   **175.** C, A, D, B;   **176.** D, A, C, B.

Best word(s) to complete a sentence

177. compensation;   **178.** performing and level;   **179.** track and with;   **180.** failing and meeting;   **181.** the and promotional;   **182.** at and compromise;   **183.** renewed and in;   **184.** rallied and from;   **185.** in and slowing;   **186.** in and margins;   **187.** to and responding;   **188.** comparatively and if;   **189.** strategy, form and from;   **190.** growth spurt and convertible;   **191.** on, actuarial and insurance;   **192.** media, nor and commercial;   **193.** cautious, akin and positions;   **194.** unable, contraction and decline;   **195.** is, growth and rates;   **196.** measures, extremely and remaining.

English usage

197. A1 and B1, Explanation: Both bits of missing text are past tense, one continuous. Saw is past tense and sitting is a continuous action;   **198.** C in, Explanation: A preposition defines a relation. For example, in the sentence 'The girl is in the shop', 'in' is a preposition. In the sentence 'The book was written by her', 'by' is the preposition;   **199.** A2 and B1, Explanation: 'Had' identifies the sentence as in the past tense so we use the 'couldn't' and 'forgotten'. 'Can't' is the present tense.;   **200.** C largest, Explanation: These are adjectives that describe the most or least in a group of similar things. My house is the smallest, your house is the largest;   **201.** A1, Explanation: A1 is correct because the speaker is concentrating at that time;   **202.** broken, Explanation: Past participles often end in -en or –ed, they are adjectives that serve as a verb in the sentence;   **203.** A1 and B2, Explanation: My brother and I went to a particular hospital so 'the' is used to identify it. My mother is in hospital does not need the term because in this case hospital is used in the general sense;   **204.** A2 and B2, Explanation: We are drawing comparisons and to do this with short words we add 'er' but for longer words we use 'more';   **205.** A3 and B3, Explanation: 'Last night' requires the past tense of the verb and the action of Sam in the park the present tense;   **206.** ideas, Explanation: A noun serves to identify the thing, place, class or person;   **207.** B was, Explanation: A sum of money is singular so we use 'was';   **208.** B later, Explanation: Comparative adjectives allow us to draw comparisons between two similar items. 'Your train was later than mine.' 'I drove further than you.';   **209.** A1 and B1, Explanation: Here 'so' is used for emphasis while 'as' is used to make a comparison;   **210.** A2 and B2, Explanation: 'In' is used for people and places, superlatives such as 'furthest' usually take the form more…or …est, eg nicest, most beautiful, but 'far' is an exception as it becomes 'furthest';   **211.** A4 and B1, Explanation: 'Must' is used to imply that something that follows is true;   **212.** cleaning, Explanation: A verb describes an action;   **213.** A2 and B1, Explanation: A verb such as 'like' is placed alongside the object, in this case animals. So it is wrong to say 'I like very much' as this separates the verb and its object;   **214.** A2 and B2, Explanation: When something changes we use the expression 'no longer' or 'any longer'. The rule is that we use 'no longer' in the middle of a sentence and 'any longer' at the end;   **215.** A1 and B3, Explanation: Both are the past tense. A2 is wrong because 'have watched' would be used to describe the present. 'I have watched a lot of television.';   **216.** A2 and B1, Explanation: We use 'in spite of' but not 'despite of', only 'despite';   **217.** A1, Explanation: 'There' is used to refer to a location, 'their' when we are referring to people or their property. After 'while' when referring to the future we use the present tense, so not 'will';   **218.** A3, B1 and C2, Explanation: The sentence states 'notes' so from the suggested answers it must be two notes, a ten pound note is a singular so pound is correct and the number of hours worked is three so we say hours plural;   **219.** A1 and B1, Explanation: We use 'until' when an action continues but we use 'by' when something happens;   **220.** A1, B2 and C2, Explanation: We use 'at' for the time of day, 'on' for the day of the week and 'in' for the month of the year;   **221.** A3 and B2, Explanation: The apology was in the past but the act of making the noise was active so we use 'making';   **222.** A2 and B1, Explanation: For people 'apostrophe s' is used; for things the 'of the' structure is usually adopted;   **223.** A1, B2, C1 and D3, Explanation: We say 'on' a plane, 'on' a bicycle, 'in' a car and 'at' a party.

Identify the correct sentence or word(s)

224. B, Explanation: B is unclear as it is not stated whether he greeted one or two people as the two job titles could be held by one person;   **225.** A and B, Explanation: 'really carefully' is correct but it does not make sense to say that 'the Police Officer was both unimpressed' unless there were two officers;   **226.** A3 and B1, Explanation: We say a friend of yours, or your friend and a friend of mine;   **227.** A and B, Explanation: 'was' is used in the singular, 'were' for a plural subject. We share between two people and among more than two;   **228.** A2 and B1, Explanation: 'to go' is passive so we use 'going', the smell was in the past so we use the past tense;   **229.** A1 and B2, Explanation: It is said that we are in a country but on a beach;   **230.** slow, Explanation: An adjective adds detail to a noun;   **231.** A1, Explanation: 'them' serves to identify which persons are left handed; it is used when referring to two or more people or things;   **232.** A3 and B3, Explanation: 'too' means higher than desired and 'enough' means as much as is necessary;   **233.** A3 and B2, Explanation: It is said that we sit 'on' the bus but we are 'at' the back of something;   **234.** 'I am doing', Explanation: This part of the sentence gives the time which is the present and it is continuous;   **235.** A3, B3 and C3, Explanation: We say get/arrived/travel etc to a place but we do not say 'to' home. For example 'go home', 'on the way home' etc;   **236.** A1, B1 and C2, Explanation: We say 'in my car' or 'by bus' and 'by car' and 'by cheque' but 'in cash';   **237.** 4 – beautiful, young, blue green, Explanation: Adjectives add detail so beautiful and young add detail to what is known about the woman and blue and green add detail to what is known about the dress;   **238.** A and B, Explanation: Both sentences misuse the meaning of the word 'unique' which means one of a kind, unlike anything else;   **239.** A2 and B3, Explanation: 'so' and 'such' serve to add emphasis; 'so' is used with adjectives and 'such' with nouns;   **240.** A4, Explanation: Adjectives such as 'long' and 'red' are normally put in the order of size then colour. We would only use 'and' if a list was formed, for example a long red and white coat;   **241.** A1 and B3, Explanation: 'who' introduces the clause that provides the extra information about where Peter lives. 'Which' and 'what' refer to objects, 'who' and 'whom' to people. We use 'which' rather than 'what' because we are referring to something already mentioned;   **242.** f themselves, Explanation: 'myself', 'my' and 'ours' are possessive pronouns. The rest are reflective but only 'themselves' is plural;   **243.** A2, B2 and C1, Explanation: 'each' and 'every' are often interchangeable but in these instances we are referring to the teams in the particular games, not every rugby team. Also, when we describe how often something occurs we use 'every';   **244.** A2 and B3, Explanation: 'much' and 'little' are used with unspecified quantities; 'much' is correct because the 'but' implies a tension with 'little'. 'Few' is used for plural subjects;   **245.** A2 and B2, Explanation: 'some' is used to make a positive point while 'any' is used in a negative situation;   **246.** A4 and B3, Explanation: When we introduce something for the first time we refer to it as 'there's'; for subsequent references 'it' is used. 'There's' is an abbreviation for 'there is'. 'Their' is used when the subject is a person, 'there' for a place.

Read a passage and evaluate a statement

Passage 1

247. C, Explanation: The passage makes no comment on how the world would be if there were no colours;   **248.** A, Explanation: 'Amalgamate' means mixture and the passage states that white light is a mix of all the wavelengths;   **249.** B, Explanation: The passage does not make this statement;   **250.** A, Explanation: The truth of this statement follows logically from the passage;   **251.** A, Explanation: The truth of this statement can be inferred from the passage.

Passage 2

252. A, Explanation: The period 1797 to 1815 totals 18 years;   **253.** A, Explanation: The passage states that Napoleon was the emperor of France which conquered much of the continent of Europe;   **254.** C, Explanation: The passage states that the French army was the most powerful but you cannot safely infer that it was also the largest;   **255.** C, Explanation: The passage states that France was at war with these kingdoms but does not say whether France won battles against them all;   **256.** B, Explanation: No date for this battle is given in the passage.

Passage 3

257. B, Explanation: The passage states that this was true traditionally but that today medicine is also concerned with prevention;   **258.** B, Explanation: The passage describes the legacy of treatments and techniques pioneered centuries ago;   **259.** A, Explanation: This is stated in the passage;   **260.** C, Explanation: The views of the author are not disclosed;   **261.** A, Explanation: The passage states that doctors use treatments of many types and gives examples of both techniques (surgery) and technologies such as radiation and vaccines.

Passage 4

262. A, Explanation: The passage states that Asia was the birthplace of civilization; **263.** C, Explanation: The passage does not provide any information on this point; **264.** A, Explanation: The passage states that the people of Asia make up over two-thirds of the world's population;   **265.** C, Explanation: The passage states that the first economies to boom were Japan, Singapore, Taiwan and South Korea. It does not say in which of these it first occurred;   **266.** A, Explanation: The passage states that Asia is the world's largest continent so the truth of this statement can be inferred.

Passage 5

267. B, Explanation: The passage states that the climate will be cooler, not the weather; **268.** A, Explanation: The passage gives examples of causes and mechanisms of climate change;   **269.** A, Explanation: The passage states that in tropical rainforests the climate remains hot and damp all the year round;   **270.** C, Explanation: The passage does not provide information on this point and it cannot be safely inferred from the passage;   **271.** A, Explanation: The passage states that the artic is cold all year and that the polar zone is the only climate zone where it is always cold.

Passage 6

272. B, Explanation: The passage describes smaller particles;   **273.** B, Explanation: The passage describes matter as being either elements or compounds;   **274.** C, Explanation: A tricky one – the passage describes molecules as atoms bonded together but it states only that atoms are held together by bonds. The means by which molecules are bonded together is not stated;   **275.** A, Explanation: This is stated in the passage;   **276.** A, Explanation: The passage states that all matter is made up of atoms including molecules and that atoms are made from these smaller particles.

Passage 7

277. C, Explanation: The passage does not provide details of which type of fraud is the most common;   **278.** C, Explanation: No details of the new measures are given in the passage;   **279.** B, Explanation: The passage states that the new measures are not yet in place;   **280.** B, Explanation: Total card fraud has reached £500 million; most but not all of this fraud is committed as a result of intercepted cards;   **281.** A, Explanation: This is clear from a careful reading of the passage.

Passage 8

282. A, Explanation: This can be readily deduced from the passage;   **283.** A, Explanation: The passage provides details of the lives and injuries saved and details the cost in terms of the environment and delays to the ambulance service;   **284.** C, Explanation: The passage does not inform us of driver attitudes;   **285.** A, Explanation: The passage states that road humps disrupt the flow of traffic;   **286.** B. Explanation: The passage does not state that this is true, only that critics claim this to be the case.

Passage 9

287. B, Explanation: The 1,000 deaths result from hospital-acquired infections; **288.** C, Explanation: The passage provides no information on how the antibiotic-resistant bacteria might have been countered in the 1950s;   **289.** B, Explanation: The passage states that the infection became established in hospitals and nursing homes since that time;   **290.** A, Explanation: The term is used to describe it in the passage; **291.** C, Explanation: The passage does not provide information on the relative severity of these conditions.

Passage 10

292. C, Explanation: The passage does not say whether or not the administrators voiced their concerns to government;   **293.** A, Explanation: The passage states that widespread fraud would discredit the electoral process but that fraud is currently rare;   **294.** A, Explanation: The passage states that recent changes to the system have led to an increased fear of fraud. So the truth of this assertion can be inferred from the passage;   **295.** A, Explanation: The passages states that checks are made but the new system may not allow sufficient time to complete them;   **296.** B, Explanation: It is not clear as the views of the author are not given.

Passage 11

297. C, Explanation: The passage does not give details of the actual record price, only the range of prices and the current price;   **298.** B, Explanation: The most efficient fields currently extract oil at these prices; the new techniques will allow for more oil to be economically extracted but the price of extraction for these techniques is not given;   **299.** A, Explanation: While it is not explicitly stated in the passage it is a reasonable assumption from reading the passage;   **300.** B, Explanation: This is not explicitly stated in the passage;   **301.** A, Explanation: The results are described as unexpected and to have led to improved forecasts of both the amount of oil and the amount that can be economically extracted. It is fair therefore to conclude that analysts were impressed by the findings.

Passage 12

302. A, Explanation: It also mentions journalists but this does not affect the truth of the statement;   **303.** B, Explanation: The passage states that solicitors only have to report suspicions of money laundering;   **304.** A, Explanation: The passage describes exceptions for all the professions, including journalists, who might break their code under order of a court;   **305.** C, Explanation: Only four professions are covered in the passage so we do not know if all professions have these codes; **306.** B, Explanation: The passage states only that they must report such injuries, not that they can be prosecuted.

Passage 13

307. A, Explanation: 80,000 by benefit officers and 44,000 by local authorities;   **308.** B, Explanation: The passage states that the new lower total was the lowest for 10 years so the level must have been lower 10 years ago;   **309.** B, Explanation: Housing benefit is also awarded to the low paid;   **310.** A, Explanation: In the passage the fall in false claims is described as spectacular;   **311.** A, Explanation: The passage states that the £½ billion drop is equivalent to 25%, so the level of fraud 12 months previously would have been £2 billion.

Passage 14

312. A, Explanation: Such growth does not occur in some parts of the developed world and the passage asked if it is realistic to assume that prices will always rise; **313.** C, Explanation: Only the views of middle class people in the United States, Spain, Ireland and the UK are detailed; we are not informed of the views of the middle classes from other countries and cannot infer this information;   **314.** B, Explanation: Homeownership would become less attractive so we might expect more people to rent not fewer;   **315.** B, Explanation: The passage states that prices have almost doubled;   **316.** A, Explanation: This is a fair summary of the passage.

Passage 15

317. B, Explanation: The process of depopulation is described as having reduced to a trickle, so it continues;   **318.** B, Explanation: Over half of the new jobs are public appointments; **319.** C, Explanation: The city of Liverpool is described this way but no information is given or can be inferred as to the relative state of the region's economy; **320.** A, Explanation: The subsidy is described as playing a significant part in attracting jobs and investment; **321.** A, Explanation: Low living and housing costs have attracted jobs and as other cities have become expensive Liverpool has become more popular.

Numerical reasoning

The key operations

Mental arithmetic

1. 3; **2.** 7; **3.** 6; **4.** 77; **5.** 6; **6.** 9; **7.** 12; **8.** 144; **9.** 8; **10.** 4; **11.** 84; **12.** 3; **13.** 5; **14.** 11; **15.** 4; **16.** 33; **17.** 7; **18.** 90; **19.** 11; **20.** 5; **21.** 6; **22.** 9; **23.** 10; **24.** 33; **25.** 4; **26.** 5; **27.** 11; **28.** 7; **29.** 42; **30.** 9; **31.** 25; **32.** 11; **33.** 8; **34.** 108; **35.** 11; **36.** 8; **37.** 7; **38.** 20; **39.** 8; **40.** 4; **41.** 6; **42.** 4; **43.** 6; **44.** 8; **45.** 4; **46.** 18; **47.** 11; **48.** 9; **49.** 8; **50.** 32; **51.** 6; **52.** 9; **53.** 64; **54.** 11; **55.** 7; **56.** 30; **57.** 9; **58.** 11; **59.** 48; **60.** 9; **61.** 7; **62.** 36; **63.** 12; **64.** 3; **65.** 1, 2, 3, 6, 9, 18, Explanation: $1 \times 18 = 18$, $2 \times 9 = 18$, $3 \times 6 = 18$, $9 \times 2 = 18$, $18 \times 1 = 18$; **66.** 1, 3, 9, 27, Explanation: 1×27, 3×9, 9×3, 27×1; **67.** 1, 11, Explanation: 11 is a prime number, ie a number whose factors are only 1 and itself; **68.** 1, 2, 11, 22, Explanation: 1×22, 2×11, 11×2, 22×1; **69.** 1, 2, 3, 4, 6, 9, 12, 18 36, Explanation: 1×36, 2×18, 3×12, 4×9, 6×6, 9×4, 12×3, 18×2, 36×1; **70.** 4, Explanation: They are 1, 2, 4, 5, 10 and 20; **71.** 8, Explanation: They are 1, 2, 4, 7, 8, 14, 28 and 56; **72.** 2, Explanation: 19 is a prime number; **73.** 1, 2, 3, 4, 5, 6 10, 12, 15, 20, 30, 60; **74.** 4, Explanation: They are 1, 2, 7, 14; **75.** 1, 2, 3, 6, 7, 14, 21, 42; **76.** 2, Explanation: 37 is a prime number; **77.** 1, 2, 4, 8, 16; **78.** 9, Explanation: 1, 2, 3, 4, 6, 8, 12, 16, 24, 48; **79.** 1, 2, 3, 4, 6, 8, 12, 24; **80.** 6, Explanation: 1, 2, 4, 8, 16, 32; **81.** 4, Explanation: 1, 2, 17, 34; **82.** 4, Explanation: This is the whole number that divides exactly into both figures. $4 \times 2 = 8$ and $4 \times 5 = 20$; **83.** 4, Explanation: The following whole numbers divide exactly into both these numbers: 1, 2, 3 and 6; **84.** 7, Explanation: $7 \times 3 = 21$ $7 \times 7 = 49$; **85.** 3, Explanation: They are 1, 2 and 4; **86.** 1,270, Explanation: These are easy but be sure that you can do them by moving the decimal place to the right by the number of 0s for multiplication; **87.** 163; **88.** 3.76, Explanation: Move the decimal point by the number of 0s to the left; **89.** 90,600; **90.** 0.024; **91.** 9.6; **92.** 0.01502; **93.** 3,002; **94.** 0.007; **95.** 3; **96.** 18,400, Explanation: First multiply by the 2 and then move the decimal place. $920 \times 2 = 1840 \times 10 = 18,400$; **97.** 3, Explanation: First divide by 100 and then by 4, $12 \div 4 = 3$; **98.** 210,000, Explanation: $3 \times 7 = 21$, $1,000 \times 10 = 10,000$, $21 \times 10,000 = 210,000$; **99.** 800, Explanation: $48 \div 6 = 8$, $1,000 \div 10 = 100$, $8 \times 100 = 800$; **100.** 180,000, Explanation: $6 \times 3 = 18$, $100 \times 100 = 10,000$, $18 \times 10,000 = 180,000$

Percentages

Changing fractions to decimals

101. 20%, Explanation: $100 \div 5 = 20 \times 1 = 20$;   **102.** 25%, Explanation: $100 \div 4 = 25 \times 1 = 25$;   **103.** 11.1%, Explanation: $100 \div 9 = 11.11$ (recurring) so treat it as $11.1 \times 1 = 11.1$; **104.** 8.3%, Explanation: $100 \div 12 = 8.333 = 8.3 \times 1 = 8.3$;   **105.** 12.5%, Explanation: $100 \div 8 = 12.5 \times 1 = 12.5$;   **106.** 6.25%, Explanation: $100 \div 16 = 6.25 \times 1 = 6.25$; **107.** 66.6%, Explanation: $100 \div 3 = 33.3 \times 2 = 66.6$;   **108.** 60%, Explanation: $100 \div 5 = 20 \times 3 = 60$;   **109.** 37.5%, Explanation: $100 \div 16 = 6.25 \times 6 = 37.5$;   **110.** 62.5%, Explanation: $100 \div 8 = 12.5 \times 5 = 62.5$;   **111.** 66.6%, Explanation: First reduce the fraction to its lowest term. $4/6 = 2/3$, $100 \div 3 = 33.3 \times 2 = 66.6$;   **112.** 75%, Explanation: $6/8 = 3/4$, $100 \div 4 = 25 \times 3 = 75$;   **113.** 80%, Explanation: $12/15 = 4/5$, $100 \div 5 = 20 \times 4 = 80$;   **114.** 20%, Explanation: $4/20 = 1/5$, $100 \div 5 = 20 \times 1 = 20$; **115.** 37.5%, Explanation: $9/24 = 3/8$, $100 \div 8 = 12.5 \times 3 = 37.5$;   **116.** 40%, Explanation: $8/20 = 2/5$, $100 \div 5 = 20 \times 2 = 40$;   **117.** 18.75%, Explanation: $6/32 = 3/16$, $100 \div 16 = 6.25 \times 3 = 18.75$;   **118.** 75%, Explanation: $21/28 = \frac{3}{4}$, $100 \div 4 = 25 \times 3 = 75$;   **119.** 31.25%, Explanation: $25/80 = 5/16$, $100 \div 16 = 6.25 \times 5 = 31.25$

Changing between decimals and percentages

120. 50%, Explanation: $0.5 \times 100 = 50$;   **121.** 20%, Explanation: $0.2 \times 100 = 20$; **122.** 60%, Explanation: $0.6 \times 100 = 60$;   **123.** 0.25, Explanation: $25 \div 100 = 0.25$; **124.** 40%, Explanation: $0.4 \times 100 = 40$;   **125.** 0.9, Explanation: $90 \div 100 = 0.9$; **126.** 35%, Explanation: $0.35 \times 100 = 35$;   **127.** 0.05, Explanation: $0.5 \div 100 = 0.05$; **128.** 72%, Explanation: $0.72 \times 100 = 72$;   **129.** 0.024, Explanation: $2.4 \div 100 = 0.024$; **130.** 42.5%, Explanation: $0.425 \times 100 = 42.5$;   **131.** 160%, Explanation: $1.6 \times 100 = 160$; **132.** 33.3%, Explanation: $0.333 \times 100 = 33.3$;   **133.** 1.2, Explanation: $120 \div 100 = 1.2$; **134.** 0.005, Explanation: $0.5 \div 100 = 0.005$

Expressing values as percentage

135. 60%, Explanation: $30/50 = 3/5$, $100 \div 5 = 20 \times 3 = 60$;   **136.** 25%, Explanation: $10/40 = \frac{1}{4}$, $100 \div 4 = 25 \times 1 = 25$;   **137.** 40%, Explanation: $100 \div 5 = 20 \times 2 = 40$; **138.** 11.1%, Explanation: $3/27 = 1/9$, $100 \div 9 = 11.1$;   **139.** 15%, Explanation: $12/80 = 3/20$, $100 \div 20 = 5 \times 3 = 15\%$;   **140.** 25%, Explanation: $4/16 = 1/4$, $100 \div 4 = 25 \times 1 = 25$;   **141.** 30%, Explanation: $12/40 = 3/10$, $100 \div 10 = 10 \times 3 = 30$; **142.** 40%, Explanation: $14/35 = 2/5$, $100 \div 5 = 20 \times 2 = 40$;   **143.** 83.5%, Explanation: $25/30 = 5/6$, $100 \div 6 = $ (16.666 so treat as) $16.7 \times 5 = 83.5$;   **144.** 80%, Explanation: Get rid of the decimal $10/12.5 = 20/25 = 4/5$, $100 \div 5 = 20 \times 4 = 80$;   **145.** 16.7%, Explanation: $0.5/3 = 1/6$, $100 \div 6 = 16.7 \times 1 = 16.7$;   **146.** 33.3%, Explanation: $0.3/0.9 = 3/9 = 1/3$, $100 \div 3 = 33.3 \times 1 = 33.3$;   **147.** 0.25%, Explanation: $0.2/80$ (multiply top and bottom by 5) $= 1/400$, $100 \div 400 = 0.25 \times 1 = 0.25$; **148.** 110%, Explanation: $3.3/3 = 33/30 = 11/10$, $100 \div 10 = 10 \times 11 = 110$; **149.** 18.75%, Explanation: $6/32 = 3/16$, $100 \div 16 = 6.25 \times 3 = 18.75$

Percentages of quantities

150. £10, Explanation: $12.5 \div 100 = 0.125$, $80 \times 0.125 = 10$; **151.** 1 hour and 15 minutes, Explanation: $25 \div 100 = 0.25 \times 300$ minutes (5 hours $\times$ 60) $= 75$ minutes $= 1$ hour 15 minutes; **152.** 4 m, Explanation: $25 \div 100 = 0.25 \times 16 = 4$; **153.** 25 pence, Explanation: $5 \div 100 = 0.05 \times 5 = 0.25$; **154.** 11 m, Explanation: $20 \div 100 = 0.2 \times 55 = 11$; **155.** 12 minutes, Explanation: 1 hour 20 minutes $= 80$ minutes, $15 \div 100 = 0.15 \times 80 = 12$; **156.** £43.20, Explanation: $12 \div 100 = 0.12 \times 360 = £43.2 = £.43.20$; **157.** 27 minutes and 30 seconds, Explanation: 3 hours 40 minutes $= 220$ minutes, $12.5 \div 100 = 0.125 \times 220 = 27.5 = 27$ minutes and 30 seconds; **158.** 31.5 m, Explanation: $45 \div 100 = 0.45 \times 70 = 31.5$; **159.** £9.18, Explanation: $45 \div 100 = 0.45 \times 20.4 = 9.18$; **160.** 45 cm, Explanation: $15 \div 100 = 0.15 \times 3 = 0.45$ metres $= 45$ cm; **161.** 7 hours and 12 minutes, Explanation: 24 hours $= 1{,}440$ minutes, $30 \div 100 = 0.3 \times 1{,}440 = 432$ minutes $\div 60 = 7.2$ hours $= 7$ hours and 12 minutes; **162.** 30m, Explanation: $12 \div 100 = 0.12 \times 250 = 30$; **163.** £271.25, Explanation: $17.5 \div 100 = 0.175 \times 1{,}550 = 271.25$; **164.** 2 hours and 9 minutes and 36 seconds, Explanation: $72 \times 60 = 4{,}320$, $3 \div 100 = 0.03$, $4{,}320 \times 0.03 = 129.6$, $129 \div 60 = 2$ hours and 9 minutes, 0.6 of a minute $= 0.6 \times 60 = 36$

Percentage increase

165. 50%, Explanation: Increase $= 10$, $10 \div 20 = 0.5 \times 100 = 50$; **166.** 20%, Explanation: $4 \div 20 = 0.2 \times 100 = 20$; **167.** 40%, Explanation: $16 \div 40 = 0.4 \times 100 = 40$; **168.** 12.5%, Explanation: $1 \div 8 = 0.125 \times 100 = 12.5$; **169.** 60%, Explanation: $3 \div 5 = 0.6 \times 100 = 60$; **170.** 25%, Explanation: $4 \div 16 = 0.25 \times 100 = 25$; **171.** 30%, Explanation: $21 \div 70 = 0.3 \times 100 = 30$; **172.** 40%, Explanation: $0.2 \div 0.5 = 0.4 \times 100 = 40$; **173.** 110%, Explanation: $22 \div 20 = 1.1 \times 100 = 110$; **174.** 300%, Explanation: $15 \div 5 = 3 \times 100 = 300$; **175.** 4%, Explanation: $4.8 \div 120 = 0.04 \times 100 = 4$; **176.** 60%, Explanation: $21.6 \div 36 = 0.6 \times 100 = 60$; **177.** 250%, Explanation: $0.25 \div 0.1 = 2.5 \times 100 = 250$; **178.** 8%, Explanation: $7.2 \div 90 = 0.08 \times 100 = 8$; **179.** 30%, Explanation: $7.5 \div 25 = 0.3 \times 100 = 30$

Percentage decrease

180. 5%, Explanation: $100 - 95 = 5$ (the decrease) $5 \div 100 = 0.05 \times 100 = 5$; **181.** 20%, Explanation: $40 - 32 = 8$, $8 \div 40 = 0.2 \times 100 = 20$; **182.** 40%, Explanation: $45 - 27 = 18$, $18 \div 45 = 0.4 \times 100 = 40$; **183.** 50%, Explanation: $72 - 36 = 36$, $36 \div 72 = 0.5$, $0.5 \times 100 = 50$; **184.** 60%, Explanation: $120 - 48 = 72$, $72 \div 120 = 0.6 \times 100 = 60$; **185.** 25%, Explanation: $12 - 9 = 3$, $3 \div 12 = 0.25 \times 100 = 25$; **186.** 75%, Explanation: $16 - 4 = 12$, $12 \div 16 = 0.75 \times 100 = 75$; **187.** 12%, Explanation: $70 - 61.6 = 8.4$, $8.4 \div 70 = 0.12 \times 100 = 12$; **188.** 40%, Explanation: $56 - 33.6 = 22.4 \div 56 = 0.4 \times 100 = 40$; **189.** 2%, Explanation: $220 - 215.6 = 4.4 \div 220 = 0.02 \times 100 = 2$; **190.** 22%, Explanation: $100 - 78 = 22 \div 100 = .22 \times 100 = 22$; **191.** 5%, Explanation: $7 - 6.65 = 0.35 \div 7 = 0.05 \times 100 = 5$; **192.** 12%, Explanation: $3.5 - 3.08 = 0.42 \div 3.5 = 0.12 \times 100 = 12$; **193.** 30%, Explanation: $25 - 17.5 = 7.5 \div 25 = 0.3 \times 100 = 30$; **194.** 12%, Explanation: $30 - 26.4 = 3.6 \div 30 = 0.12 \times 100 = 12$; **195.** 22%, Explanation: $65 - 50.7 = 14.3 \div 65 = 0.22 \times 100 = 22$

Percentage profit and loss

196. 20% profit, Explanation: 12 – 10 = £2 profit, 2 ÷ 10 = 0.2 × 100 = 20;   **197.** 10% loss, Explanation: 10 – 9 = £1 loss, 1 ÷ 10 = 0.1 × 100 = 10;   **198.** 20% loss, Explanation: 40 – 32 = 8 loss, 8 ÷ 40 = 0.2 × 100 = 20;   **199.** 40% profit, Explanation: 70 – 50 = 20 profit, 20 ÷ 50 = 0.4 × 100 = 40;   **200.** 25% profit, Explanation: 5 – 4 = 1 profit, 1 ÷ 4 = 0.25 × 100 = 25;   **201.** 12.5% loss, Explanation: 8 – 7 = 1 loss, 1 ÷ 8 = 0.125 × 100 = 12.5;   **202.** 18% loss, Explanation: 290 – 237.80 = 52.2 ÷ 290 = 0.18 × 100 = 18;   **203.** 23% loss, Explanation: 82 – 63.14 = 18.86 loss, 18.86 ÷ 82 = 0.23 × 100 = 23; **204.** 25% profit, Explanation: 25 –20 = 5 profit, 5 ÷ 20 = 0.25 × 100 = 25;   **205.** 3% loss, Explanation: 370 – 358.90 = 11.1 loss, 11.1 ÷ 370 = 0.03 × 100 = 3;   **206.** 32% profit, Explanation: 66 – 50 = 16 profit, 16 ÷ 50 = 0.32 × 100 = 32;   **207.** 80% loss, Explanation: 12 – 2.4 = 9.6 loss, 9.6 ÷ 12 = 0.8 × 100 = 80;   **208.** 6% loss, Explanation: 6.5 – 6.11 = 0.39 loss, 0.39 ÷ 6.50 = 0.06 × 100 = 6;   **209.** 32% profit, Explanation: 132 – 100 = 32 profit, 32 ÷ 100 = 0.32 x 100 = 32;   **210.** 15% profit, Explanation: 5.75 – 5.00 = 0.75 profit, 0.75 ÷ 5 = 0.15 × 100 = 15

Sequencing

211. 12, Explanation: 5 is added each step in the sequence;   **212.** 34, Explanation: 8 is taken away each step in the sequence;   **213.** 1, Explanation: The previous sum is multiplied by 6 each step;   **214.** 35, Explanation: Add 5 each step;   **215.** 27, Explanation: Divide the previous sum by 3;   **216.** 37.5, Explanation: Multiply the previous sum by 2 each step;   **217.** 11, Explanation: The sequence decreases by 4 each step;   **218.** 27, Explanation: The previous sum is multiplied by 3 each step;   **219.** 522, Explanation: Add 87 each step;   **220.** 67.5, Explanation: Divide the previous sum by 3 each step;   **221.** 25, Explanation: Add the previous two values to find the next, ie 9 + 16 = 25;   **222.** 159, Explanation: Add 17 each step;   **223.** 251, Explanation: Minus 26 each step;   **224.** 100, Explanation: Divide the previous sum by 2.5 each step;   **225.** 70, Explanation: Add 14 each step;   **226.** 0.5, Explanation: The previous two values are added together each step, so to find the first value minus 2 from 2.5 = 0.5;   **227.** 1,504, Explanation: Add 101 each step;   **228.** 1, Explanation: Divide the previous sum by 10 each step;   **229.** –13, Explanation: Take away 71 each step;   **230.** 60, Explanation: Add together the previous two values, 21 + 39 = 60;   **231.** 4, Explanation: Multiply each sum by 0.4;   **232.** –56, Explanation: Minus 22 each step;   **233.** 12.5, Explanation: Multiply the previous sum by 5 each step;   **234.** 31, Explanation: Add the previous two values to find the next, 8 + 23 = 31;   **235.** 71, Explanation: It's a bit of a trick – 34 is added at each step from the starting number 107, but the sequence of numbers is then presented in a misleading way. It should look like 107, 141, 175, 209 but it has been presented as 10, 71, 41, 17, 52, 09;   **236.** 18, Explanation: Multiply the two previous values 3 × 6 = 18;   **237.** 60, Explanation: Each step the previous sum is multiplied by 1.5;   **238.** 999, Explanation: 333 is added each step in the series ;   **239.** 173, Explanation: Add together the previous two values 81 + 92 = 173;   **240.** 62, Explanation: Minus 12 each step starting with 198, but the sequence has been presented as 19, 81, 86, 17, 41, 62 instead of 198, 186 etc;   **241.** 3, Explanation: Multiply the previous two values to get the next, $3 \times 1 = 3$;   **242.** 0.48, Explanation: Multiply by 0.2 each step;   **243.** 17, Explanation: Start with 91 and add 29 each step and misrepresent the series 91, 120, 149, 178, 207 as 91, 12, 01, 49, 17, 8,207;   **244.** 25, Explanation: The sequence is that of the first 6 whole square numbers (numbers multiplied by themselves), $5 \times 5 = 25$;   **245.** 13, Explanation: The sequence is the first 8 prime numbers (a number with only 1 and itself as factors);   **246.** 80, Explanation: Starting from 800 minus 20 each step and misrepresent the sequence 800, 780, 760, 740 as 80, 07, 80, 76, 07, 40;   **247.** 15:20, Explanation: The sequence comprises equivalent ratios starting with the lowest expression;   **248.** 4, Explanation: Multiply the two previous terms each step to get the second value, divide 8 by $2 = 4$;   **249.** 108, Explanation: Multiply the previous sum by 6 each step, $6 \times 18 = 108$;   **250.** 53, Explanation: The sequence is the first six whole square numbers, 1, 4, 9, 16, 25, 36, presented in a misleading way;   **251.** 51, Explanation: Start with 155 and add 15 each step; the sequence is then presented in a misleading way;   **252.** 99, Explanation: Add the previous two sums, $41 + 58 = 99$;   **253.** 192, Explanation: Multiply the two previous terms, $8 \times 24 = 192$;   **254.** 49, Explanation: Divide the previous sum by 7 each step;   **255.** 49, Explanation: The sequence is that of the square numbers starting with $6 \times 6 = 36$, $7 \times 7 = 49$;   **256.** 1, Explanation: The sequence is the whole number factors of 12;   **257.** 117, Explanation: 13 is added to the previous sum each step;   **258.** 3, Explanation: Each number is followed by its square root;   **259.** 32, Explanation: 2 is raised to the power of 2^2–2^7; missing is 2 to the power of $5 = 2 \times 2 \times 2 \times 2 \times 2 = 32$;   **260.** 49, Explanation: Add the previous two values to get the next, $11 + 38 = 49$;   **261.** 4:8, Explanation: The sequence starts with a ratio in its lowest form and is followed by the next equivalent;   **262.** 3, Explanation: The sequence is a list of the whole number factors of 15; missing is $3 \times 5 = 15$;   **263.** 1,000, Explanation: The sequence is that of the cubed numbers in the range 6^3–10^3; missing is $10 \times 10 \times 10 = 1,000$;   **264.** 12, Explanation: Multiply the previous step by 4, $3 \times 4 = 12$;   **265.** 112, Explanation: Add 14 each step in the sequence;   **266.** 283, Explanation: Starting with 22, it is the sequence of even numbers presented in a misleading way;   **267.** 81, Explanation: The sequence is 3 raised to the powers 3^2–3^6; missing is $3^4 = 3 \times 3 \times 3 \times 3 = 81$;   **268.** 0.1, Explanation: The previous sum is multiplied by 0.2 each step;   **269.** 29, Explanation: Add the previous two values to find the next;   **270.** 100, Explanation: The sequence is the range of numbers 12^2– 8^2; missing is $10^2 = 10 \times 10 = 100$;   **271.** 7, Explanation: This is the list of whole number factors of 14; missing is $7 \times 2 = 14$;   **272.** 256, Explanation: Multiply the previous two sums to get the next, $8 \times 32 = 256$;   **273.** 256, Explanation: The sequence is the value of 4^2–4^5; missing is $4^4 = 4 \times 4 \times 4 \times 4 = 256$;   **274.** 108, Explanation: Divide the previous sum by 3 each step;   **275.** 123, Explanation: Starting with 19, it is the sequence of odd numbers presented in a misleading way;   **276.** 0.25, Explanation: Multiply by 12 each step to find the first value; divide 3 by $12 = 0.25$;   **277.** 025, Explanation: You should be able to recognize these by now; starting with 5 it is the sequence of multiples of 5 presented in a misleading way;   **278.** 4, Explanation: It is the sequence of whole number factors of 16; missing is $4 \times 4 = 16$;   **279.** 80, Explanation: The previous sum is divided by 4 each step;   **280.** 125, Explanation: The sequence is that of the values 5^2–5^5; missing is 5^3, $5 \times 5 \times 5 = 125$;   **281.** 64, Explanation: 8 is added each step;   **282.** 0.2, Explanation: It is the sequence of first 5 whole number reciprocals of 1 (that do not produce a recurring number), ie $1 \div 2 = 0.5$, $1 \div 4 = 0.25$, $1 \div 5 = 0.2$, $1 \div 8 = 0.125$, $1 \div 10 = 0.1$; **283.** 3, Explanation: It is a list of the whole number factors of 18; 3 is missing, $3 \times 6 = 18$; **284.** 121, Explanation: This is a sequence of the multiples of 3 beginning with 3 and presented in a misleading way; **285.** 11, Explanation: It is the sequence of prime numbers in descending order in the range 19–7

Number problems

286. D, Explanation: $55 \times 5 = 275$, $110 \times 2 = 220$, $275 + 220 = £4.95$; **287.** B, Explanation: $1.20 \times 6 = 7.20$; **288.** C, Explanation: $30 \times 60 = 1,800$; **289.** B, Explanation: $40 \times 6 = 240$, $240 \times 12 = 2,880$ (you might do this second sum like this: $24 \times 12 = 2$ $(12 \times 12) = 2 \times 144 = 288$ but then put the 0 back $= 2,880$); **290.** A, Explanation: $12 \times 18 = 216$ (a quick way to calculate this is $10 \times 18 = 180$, $2 \times 18 = 36$, $180 + 36 = 216$). $216 - 200 = 16$; **291.** C, Explanation: $200 \times 15 = 3,000$ ($2 \times 15 = 30$, add the $00 = 3,000$); **292.** A, Explanation: $15 \times 75 = 1,125$ pence or 11.25 (a quick way to do this is to work out $10 \times 75 = 750$, $5 \times 75 = 375$, add then together $= 1,125$); **293.** B, Explanation: $9 = 27$ so each box weighs 300 gm ($2,700$ gm $\div 9$), $300 \times 4 = 1,200$ gm $= 1.2$ kg; **294.** D, Explanation: Work out the rate for one minute, 2,000 divided by 8, and multiply by $9 = 2,250$; **295.** A, Explanation: Work out the cost per 100 gm, $750 \div 3 = 250$ per 100 gm, $2,600 \div 10 = 260$ per 100 gm; **296.** C, Explanation: Remember to convert the shoes to pairs of shoes, 192 shoes $= 96$ pairs, $96 \div 8 = 12$ (you should know that $12 \times 8 = 96$); **297.** C, Explanation: $40 \times 15 = 600$ ($4 \times 15 = 60$ then add the 0); **298.** A, Explanation: Work out the cost of 5 pencils, $180 \div 10 = 18$ for 5, $14 \times 5 = 70$ so $18 \times 14 =$ cost of 70 pencils $= 252$; **299.** D, Explanation: $132 \div 6 = 22$ (work this out quickly by breaking the 132 down, ie $10 \times 6 = 60$, $20 \times 6 = 120$, add $12 = 132$, so $22 \times 6 = 132$); $22 \times 4 = 88$; **300.** C, Explanation: $6,000 \div 30 = 200$ ($6 \div 2 = 3$, $1,000 \div 10 = 100$), $200 \times 5 = 1,000$; **301.** D, Explanation: Rental $= £9$ per quarter $= £3$ per month, so £11 is spent on calls $(14 - 3)$ each month, $11 \times 12 = 132$; **302.** B, Explanation: $0.70 \times 250 =$ monthly cost of the cover $= 175.00 \times 12$ to get the annual cost $= £2,100$; **303.** D, Explanation: $5.20 \times 35 = 182$, $5.2 \times 1.5 = 7.8$ (hourly overtime rate), $7.8 \times 5 = 39$, $182 + 39 = 221$; **304.** A, Explanation: $18 \times 16 = 288 + 29 = 317$; **305.** B, Explanation: $60 \div 5 = 12$, $1.20 \times 12 = 14.40$ (cost of gas over 60-day period) + standing charge $0.9 \times 60 = 5.40$, $14.40 + 5.40 = 19.80$; **306.** B, Explanation: You need to express one number as a percentage of another, so treat the first number as a fraction of the second and multiply the result by 100. $30/500 = 3/50$, $100 \div 50 = 2 \times 3 = 6$; **307.** D, Explanation: $52/80 = 13/20$, $100 \div 20 = 5 \times 13 = 65$; **308.** C, Explanation: $18/60 = 3/10$, $100 \div 10 = 10 \times 3 = 30$; **309.** D, Explanation: $432/720 = 3/5$, $100 \div 5 = 20$, $20 \times 3 = 60$; **310.** C, Explanation: $9.68/88 = 968/8800 = 11/100$ (hcf 88), $100 \div 100 = 1 \times 11 = 11$; **311.** D, Explanation: Don't be put off; if you are not allowed to use a calculator then the maths will be straightforward! $487.50/640 = 48,750/65,000 = 4,875/6,500 = ¾$ (hcf 1,625), $100 \div 4 = 25 \times 3 = 75$; **312.** A, Explanation: $120/4,000 = 12/400 = 3/100$ (hcf4) $3/100 = 3\%$; **313.** C, Explanation: $63/420 = 3/20$ (hcf21), $100 \div 20 = 5 \times 3 = 15$; **314.** D, Explanation: $126/6,300 = 2/100$ (you should be able to see this straight away as $1\% = 63$ so $2\% =$

126), 2/100 =2%;   **315.** B, Explanation: 750 = 100, 1% = 750/100 = 7.5 × 4 = 30;   **316.** C, Explanation: 3 hours = 180 minutes, 100% = 180, 1% = 180/100 = 1.8, 1.8 × 15 = 27;   **317.** D, Explanation: You should be able to see this straight away, 600 = 100%, 1% = 600/100 = 6 × 12.5 = 75;   **318.** A, Explanation: Another easy one, 400 = 100%, 1% = 400/100 = 4, 4 × 9 = 36;   **319.** C, Explanation: 2,400 = 100% 1% = 2,400/100 = 24 × 2.5 = 60, 2,400 + 60 = 2,460;   **320.** B, Explanation: 14 = 100%, 1% = 14/100 = 0.14, 0.14 × 40 = 5.6, 14 + 5.6 = 19.6;   **321.** C, Explanation: 620 = 100%, 1% = 620/100 = 6.2 × 3 = 18.6; **322.** C, Explanation: 3,550 = 100%, 1% = 3,550/100 = 35.5 × 20 = 710, 3,550 − 710 = 2,840; **323.** A, Explanation: 4 hours 30 minutes = 270 minutes = 100%, 1% = 270/100 = 2.7, 2.7 × 5 = 13.5 minutes, 270 − 13 minutes 30 seconds = 4 hours 16 minutes and 30 seconds; **324.** C, Explanation: 103% = 3,605, 1% = 3,605/103 = 35/1 × 100 = 3,500;   **325.** A, Explanation: 100% = 7,000, 1% = 7,000/100 = 70 × 8 = 560, 7,000 + 560 = 7,560;   **326.** B, Explanation: 4,300 =100%, 1% = 4,300/100 = 43 × 4 = 172, 4,300 − 172 = 4,128;   **327.** B, Explanation: Blue party obtained 30,000 + 8%, 1% = 30,000/100 = 300, 300 × 8 = 2,400, 30,000 + 2,400 = 32,400 votes;   **328.** D, Explanation: Red party received 22,000 − 18%, 100% = 22,000, 1% = 22,000/100 = 220, 220 × 18 = 3,960, 22,000 − 3960 = 18,040 votes; **329.** B, Explanation: 92% = 552, 1% = 552/92 = 6, 8 × 6 = 48, 552 + 48 = 600;   **330.** A, Explanation: The length of metal was 2% longer before it was cooled. 2% of 1 m = 2 cm so 2% of 3 m = 6 cm so the original length was 306 cm;   **331.** A, Explanation: 300 m = 125%, 1% = 300/125 = 12/5 = 22/5 or 2.4, 2.4 × 100 = 240;   **332.** B, Explanation: 108% = 6.75, 1% = 675/10,800 = 1/16 (hcf 675) = 0.0625 × 100 = 6.25;   **333.** C, Explanation: yr 1 6,000 × 88/100 = 60 × 88 = 5,380, yr 2 5,280 × 88/100 = 52.8 × 88 = 4,646.40;   **334.** D, Explanation: yr 1 18,000 × 105% = 18,000 + 5 × 180 = 18,900, yr 2 18,900 × 105% = 18,900 + 5 × 189 = 19,845;   **335.** C, Explanation: It is an easy one so long as you sort out the task: 8 seconds as an improvement on the original time, original time = 8 + 12 = 20, so we must find 8 as a percentage of 20, 20 =100, 1 = 5%, 8 = 40%;   **336.** A, Explanation: 100% = 800 so we need to establish what 300 increase represents. 100 ÷ 800 = 0.125 × 300 = 37.5;   **337.** D, Explanation: It is an easy question and you will find some in real tests and not just at the start, so keep going if you hit a more difficult patch in a real test as they are often followed by easier questions. 2,000 loss / 8,000 × 100 = ¼ × 100 = 25; **338.** C, Explanation: Profit = 8% of 25, 100% = 25, 1% = 25/100, 8% = 25/100 × 8 = ¼ × 8 = 2, selling price = 27;   **339.** B, Explanation: Loss = 4% of 120,000, 1% = 120,000/100 = 1,200, 4% = 1,200 × 4 = 4,800, purchase price = 120,000 + 4,800 = 124,800;   **340.** A, Explanation: Profit on 12 eggs = 15 × 12 − 150 = 30, % profit = 30/150 × 100 = 1/5 × 100 = 0.2 × 100 = 20;   **341.** C, Explanation: It's easy once you sort out your grams and kilos. 1 kg = 10 × 100 gm, profit = 60 × 10 − 300 = 300, % profit = 300/300 × 100 = 100; **342.** D, Explanation: Purchase price = 20 × 2.5 = 50, so loss of 50 − 42 made, % loss = 8/50 × 100 = 0.16 × 100 = 16;   **343.** D, Explanation: Loss = 500,000 − 515,000 = 15,000, % loss = 15,000/500,000 × 100 = 15/500 × 100 = 1,500/ 500 = 3;   **344.** D, Explanation: Profit = 120 − 10 = 110, % profit = 110/10 × 100 = 11 × 100 = 1,100%, but this is a net profit and all the other costs of the establishment must also be recovered.

Personality questionnaires

Your approach to decision making

1. Explanation: Disagreement might be appropriate if applying for a company that has a hierarchical style and for a non-managerial position. Strong disagreement would only be appropriate for candidates for executive positions;   **2.** Explanation: Employers would consider this an important question and they may not want to employ someone who disagreed as they may be unable to separate their personal views from those that represent the best interest of the organization;   **3.** Explanation: Agreement might be appropriate for applicants to professional roles or one where someone is expected to bring stature;   **4.** Explanation: Agreement might suit a position where you work unsupervised or a role where someone risk-averse is wanted;   **5.** Explanation: Agreement would be expected for a role where team working is essential and where policy formulation is a key activity. Consistent responses would be expected with questions 1 and 2;   **6.** Explanation: Agreement would suggest a numerate candidate for a position in a financial or analytical department. An all-round candidate might disagree;   **7.** Explanation: If applying for a policy or managerial role then disagreement would be expected;   **8.** Explanation: Disagreement might suggest experience of the practical realities of business, strong agreement might suggest an over-cautious style;   **9.** Explanation: Agreement suggests a candidate happy to work in a hierarchical organization and if that is the type of organization to which you are applying then it is the best response;   **10.** Explanation: Most employers would expect a candidate to disagree with this statement. A new employee with relevant experience or professional status would hold very valid views;   **11.** Explanation: Agreement risks the impression of a candidate unused to collective decisions and team working; **12.** Explanation: Some employers would like a candidate who agreed, perhaps in a highly competitive field, but others might fear the person was too strong a personality and would fit badly in an existing team.

Communicating with others

13. Explanation: Agreement suggests a candidate suitable for a customer-facing role and a sales-oriented, ambitious candidate;   **14.** Explanation: Agreement but not strong agreement would suggest a candidate able to show sensitivity to others;   **15.** Explanation: Agreement suggests someone uninterested in sales, and a strong preference in formulating strategy rather than its implementation;   **16.** Explanation: Agreement suggests suitability for many modern-day managerial positions. Disagreement would risk the suggestion that when under pressure the candidate was unable to maintain good relations with colleagues;   **17.** Explanation: Only agree strongly with this statement if the employer is seeking this quality, otherwise you risk giving the impression of a candidate who will be hard to manage and a potential liability when dealing with colleagues and customers;

18. Explanation: Agreement would suggest someone not suited to team working; **19.** Explanation: Disagreement would be expected of an all-round candidate and anyone applying for a managerial role. Agreement would be acceptable for a candidate for a policy formation role;   **20.** Explanation: Disagreement with this statement would be expected; most employers would consider being opinionated at work as always a bad thing;   **21.** Explanation: Agreement would be expected for any role responsible for the communication of policy or the management of staff or change;   **22.** Explanation: Agreement might risk the impression of an employee who lacks commitment or who does not work fully towards the common aims of the organization. This is not an approach an employer would value in someone whom they have not yet employed;   **23.** Explanation: Agreement would support a candidate aware of the importance of relationships, personality and communication;   **24.** Explanation: Many employers are seeking staff who adopt this approach to team motivation and management. It would therefore be something with which to agree strongly if you are confident the organization values this approach;   **25.** Explanation: A bit of a trick question and, perhaps surprisingly, many questionnaires include such questions. To agree suggests a self-criticism but disagreement risks the impression that you do not recognize fully the value of lateral thinking and new ways of working. In some roles, such as strategy and senior management, agreement would be expected.

Your approach to planning

26. Explanation: Agreement suggests a strong proactive approach and an aversion to risk. These are qualities some employers value highly;   **27.** Explanation: Strong agreement would be expected of applicants for many managerial positions; it would of course have to be supported by experience detailed on your CV;   **28.** Explanation: Agreement might be taken to suggest financial acumen, strong agreement might be taken to suggest a risk-sensitive candidate, which is not a bad thing depending on the job;   **29.** Explanation: Agreement suggests a confident, reactive approach where greatest store is placed on hard work and experience rather than policy and planning; **30.** Explanation: In some roles this may well be the case but many roles demand a compromise where maximum speed is realized with the minimum of errors; **31.** Explanation: The statement describes the two most common approaches to work and management and your prospective employer will have decided which approach they prefer. So decide how you prefer to work and indicate that preference accordingly;   **32.** Explanation: An applicant for an all-round position would disagree but a specialist in sales or another customer-facing role who agreed might be exactly what an employer is looking for;   **33.** Explanation: Some industries have highly developed regulations and detailed procedures that staff are expected to follow. If you are applying for a position in such a company then avoid any impression that you find those regulations inappropriate;   **34.** Explanation: Ambiguity is a fact of life in many roles. Yet people have to make good decisions despite that uncertainty. If the role to which you apply is one in which vagueness is a part of working life then respond accordingly;   **35.** Explanation: Most employers would not like a candidate to indicate that they find an essential part of most roles demeaning; **36.** Explanation: Agreement might be interpreted as suggesting a candidate who is inflexible and unwilling to work as part of a team with collective responsibility to get the job done;   **37.** Explanation: Delegation is a key skill expected in most demanding roles. Many employers might be concerned that an employee who does not delegate will not cope at very busy times.

Managing people and resources

38. Explanation: Agreement would suggest someone who is very sales-oriented but it would also risk the interpretation that they lack sufficient awareness of the need to maintain margins and cost controls;   **39.** Explanation: Every employer wants to know as soon as something goes seriously wrong, so most would expect prospective employees to agree with this statement;   **40.** Explanation: Strong agreement might be expected of someone in a financial or purchasing role or a managerial position. Agreement would perhaps be expected of all employees;   **41.** Explanation: Agreement would suggest someone able to deal sensitively with colleagues and clients and be a good team player;   **42.** Explanation: An employer seeking a hands-on manager will be looking for agreement with this statement but practitioners of other styles of management may disagree;   **43.** Explanation: Look for constancy of answer with the last question. It is possible to agree or disagree with both but they can be taken to represent aspects of different styles of management and in your responses you should try to give as clear an indication as possible of your preferred style; **44.** Explanation: Agreement would suggest someone who is uncompromising in their commitment to a client-focused approach and this might well support an application for such a role but it would not be well received if management of people formed a significant part of the job;   **45.** Explanation: Another slightly tricky statement. Strong agreement might suggest a frustration with the widespread culture of targets and performance management and this could count against your application.

Motivating yourself and others

46. Explanation: This is a statement that most employers would want you to agree with. Do not worry about admitting to faults; after all, none of us is perfect; **47.** Explanation: A self-confident applicant who recognizes the importance of continued personal development would agree with this statement. It would help create a winning impression with most employers;   **48.** Explanation: An independent-minded employee might agree but take care not to suggest that you might be difficult to manage or reluctant to accept the authority of others to set the criteria against which your performance might be judged;   **49.** Explanation: Agreement might suggest a candidate wanting a challenge and happy to work to achieve ambitious targets;   **50.** Explanation: Agreement suggests an empowering style of management and an acceptance of the value of performance management techniques;

51. Explanation: Be careful not to agree with too many statements that begin 'above all else' or 'I most want' as it implies it is a very significant issue for you and one the employer might or might not be looking for. Agreement would suggest a very ambitious candidate and that would please many employers but not all;   **52.** Explanation: A large salary, the latest mobile phone or computer do not motivate all employees. The mission of some organizations is social or altruistic and such employers may prefer to employ candidates who agree with this statement. But be careful not to agree too strongly because many roles, while contributing to a worthy objective, do not afford the post holder a clear perspective of what is being achieved and the employer may fear that the candidate has unrealistic expectations;   **53.** Explanation: This is exactly what some employers expect and like of a candidate. Others, however, might be frightened off by such up-front ambition;   **54.** Explanation: Agree with this only if the role to which you have applied offers it, but most do not and an employer might worry that they cannot meet the aspirations of the candidate otherwise;   **55.** Explanation: Meritocracy means a place of work where people are given responsibility or selected according to merit. Many organizations consider themselves meritocracies;   **56.** Explanation: Agreement suggests that you will bring a different perspective to a role so you should only agree if this is the case and this is what the employer is looking for.

Features of your ideal role

57. Explanation: The question implies a high-pressure role and someone who can cope well in such an environment. So only agree if you want such a role and will thrive in it;   **58.** Explanation: Not all roles offer the opportunity to get stuck in and sort out a mess or see off a threat. Most employers are looking for someone to build on success or to continue the achievements of the past;   **59.** Explanation: Most employees would consider no distractions to be rather a luxury because in the real workplace distractions come thick and fast and still you have to get the job done. An employer might fear that they cannot guarantee a minimum of distractions and they might therefore reject a candidate who strongly agreed with this statement;   **60.** Explanation: Some employers want managers who are really hands on and some roles need this level of intervention, but not all, so be sure this sort of statement truly describes your preferred style of working and is what the role needs and what the employer is looking for;   **61.** Explanation: Unfortunately, this style of working does come with some territories and if you work in one of them then you will agree with this statement;   **62.** Explanation: Many of us do, but it would perhaps be unwise to make such a negative point as it would do nothing to support your application;   **63.** Explanation: The first part of the statement is fine and something many employers value, but they cannot guarantee that things will always go to plan and so would be concerned if an applicant indicated that they tend to get stressed under such circumstances.

Your attitude towards risk

64. Explanation: Unfortunately, it is not always true that the higher the risk the higher the return, so it would be unwise to agree with this statement; **65.** Explanation: Strong agreement might suggest someone who is risk sensitive, which may not be a bad thing; agreement may support the impression of financial acumen;   **66.** Explanation: It is a commonly held view but those working in even highly regulated industries still find room for creativity and an employer in one of these sectors might well be expecting a suitable candidate to disagree; **67.** Explanation: In some industries success is dependent on taking chances or going further than the competition, in others it is not and such an approach would be unwelcome;   **68.** Explanation: A client-focused role or sales position would suit someone who agreed with this statement but it would be a less suitable response for an all-round position;   **69.** Explanation: A team player would agree strongly with this statement and an employer who prefers a team approach will be attracted to this response;   **70.** Explanation: I do not think many employers would be unhappy with either, but in terms of risk the doubling of margins means much higher net profitability and so lower risk in the short term. But doubling the customer base would also have its attractions.

The secret of your success

71. Explanation: Some would disagree as they consider success to be dependent on, for example, collaboration or innovation rather than ruthlessness;   **72.** Explanation: If you bring energy and determination and a suitable number of years of experience then still be sure to agree with this statement;   **73.** Explanation: This is a combination of skills many employers value in a candidate for a managerial role; **74.** Explanation: Many companies put their success down to good management and team working and they want to recruit employees who can continue these traditions;   **75.** Explanation: Many employers would consider the success of their management and sales teams to be due to these skills and would only consider candidates who agreed strongly with it;   **76.** Explanation: Some people do succeed because of these qualities and some roles are advertised as ideally suited to someone who can bring drive and determination; if this applies to you and the position you are looking for then be sure to agree strongly;   **77.** Explanation: Recruiters to creative and strategic roles often place great value on this quality;   **78.** Explanation: Agreement with this statement will meet the approval of many employers and what they hope a new employee will bring to their organization.

Appropriate responses in work

79. D or E, Explanation: An employer would want every customer, even the challenging ones, to receive the same high standard of service;   **80.** D or E, Explanation: To raise your voice when discussing something at work would be considered inappropriate behaviour by most employers;   **81.** D or E, Explanation: Lying is a form of dishonesty that most employers would not approve of. To describe it as a little lie does not change this fact;   **82.** A or B, Explanation: Employers want to be kept informed of any issues that affect performance. They can then take them into consideration when deciding what to do to address underperformance;   **83.** D or E, Explanation: To agree would suggest that you can prejudge people; this is to admit that you have prejudices against certain types of people which, if displayed in work, is inappropriate;   **84.** D or E, Explanation: At work we have to keep our employer, colleagues and customers informed whether the news is good or bad. If you are unsure whether or not you should tell someone something, ask your line manager for guidance;   **85.** D or E, Explanation: An employer wants to know as soon as something of significance goes wrong; you can always report at the same time what actions you propose to correct the situation;   **86.** D or E, Explanation: Everyone in work receives direction and an employer would want employees to be at ease both receiving and giving orders;   **87.** D or E, Explanation: Danger has no place at work. If you consider something dangerous, inform your line manager immediately and help find a way of completing the task that avoids unnecessary risk;   **88.** D or E, Explanation: The correct action would be to inform the person upsetting you and, if this does not resolve the issue, your line manager. Otherwise implement the workplace grievance procedure which should be a part of your contract of employment;   **89.** A or B, Explanation: A serious issue such as bullying should be reported straight away so that it can be stopped;   **90.** D or E, Explanation: The passage implies that the joke is not appreciated by some colleagues and therefore it is inappropriate;   **91.** D or E, Explanation: Work should be organized so that both men and women can do every job equally well;   **92.** D or E, Explanation: Stealing is unacceptable no matter how little the value of the goods taken;   **93.** D or E, Explanation: If someone is not pulling their weight then we need to find out if there is a reason that can be corrected;   **94.** A or B, Explanation: Such action is likely to appease the anger of the customer;   **95.** D or E, Explanation: Employers would want to be informed if you found your workload too great;   **96.** A or B, Explanation: This behaviour would be considered good team working;   **97.** D or E, Explanation: Employers want staff who are flexible in their working practice and will help address the unexpected. Anyway, most job descriptions include a last sentence that says the employee should be willing to undertake any other reasonable task;   **98.** D or E, Explanation: It may well be of concern to the employer if it affects your ability to undertake your work safely or if it adversely impinges on your performance;   **99.** A or B, Explanation: Most health and safety policies require this and they are likely to form a part of your contract of employment;   **100.** D or E, Explanation: Arguments at work are inappropriate and to argue until you are affected physically by the event would be unacceptable to employers.

Non-verbal reasoning, mechanical comprehension and IQ tests

Features in common

1. A, Explanation: The example shapes and A all contain one dot;   **2.** B, Explanation: All three examples are quadrilaterals (4-sided shapes) and B is a trapezium and also a quadrilateral;   **3.** A, Explanation: The question shapes all have an even number of faces (in the case of a three-dimensional shape a face is a flat surface), the cylinder has 2, the box 6, the pyramid 4; only A, the star, also has an even number (10);   **4.** C, Explanation: All the question shapes are constructed from equilateral triangles (triangles with 3 sides equal in length); only shape C shares this quality;   **5.** A, Explanation: These shapes are called nets and some, if folded, would form a solid object. All the question shapes, if cut out and folded, could form a cube; only suggested answer A would also do this;   **6.** C, Explanation: All the question shapes have dots which total a multiple of 3: 9, 3, 6. C has 12 dots and so is the only suggested answer that also has a total number that is a multiple of 3;   **7.** B, Explanation: All 3 question shapes have an odd total number of dots, 3, 5 and 5. Only B also has an odd number of dots, 3;   **8.** A, Explanation: The question shapes are all divided by a line from top left to right; only A shares this quality;   **9.** A, Explanation: Both question shapes contain 3 triangles; only A shares this quality;   **10.** C, Explanation: In the question shapes the outer arrows point in an anticlockwise direction while the inner arrows point clockwise. Only shape C shares this quality;   **11.** B, Explanation: Both question shapes have in common the fact that if you subtract the top number of dots from the bottom number the remainder is 3. Only shape B also has this quality;   **12.** C, Explanation: Both question shapes are divided into five triangles, as is shape C;   **13.** B, Explanation: The first question shape numbers 16 squares of which 4 (¼) are shaded and the second numbers 12 squares of which 3 are shaded and also ¼ are shaded. Suggested answer B also has ¼ of its squares shaded;   **14.** B, Explanation: The question shapes have only a single shaded circle in common and only shape B also contains one shaded circle;   **15.** C, Explanation: The question shapes are both made up of 11 shapes, as is suggested answer C;   **16.** B, Explanation: Both question shapes have shaded circles at the start and end of the line, as does suggested answer B;   **17.** B, Explanation: The two question shapes have two horizontal and three or more vertical surfaces. B is the only suggested answer that has more vertical than horizontal surfaces;   **18.** A, Explanation: The sum of the dots in each of the two question shapes is a prime number, as is 7, the number of dots on suggested answer A;   **19.** C, Explanation: Both question shapes have internal angles that add up to 180°; the two angles of C also add up to 180°;   **20.** B, Explanation: Both question shapes include two triangles, as does suggested answer B;   **21.** A, Explanation: The two question shapes both comprise 24 sides, as does the shapes making up suggested answer A;   **22.** A, Explanation: Both question shapes have rotational symmetry (they look the same when rotated); only A also has this quality;   **23.** B, Explanation: Both question shapes have a consistent cross-section (this is used to calculate their volumes); the cross-sections of A and C are not consistent but B's is; **24.** A, Explanation: The number of dots in both question shapes total 6, as does suggested answer A; **25.** C, Explanation: The question shapes are related in that the second is an enlargement of the first by the scale factor of 2. Suggested answer C is related to the question shapes because if enlarged by a scale factor of 2 it would be identical to the smaller of the question triangles; **26.** A, Explanation: Both question shapes have one line of symmetry (where a line can be drawn through the shape and both sides are identical). A also shares this quality whereas N has no lines of symmetry and H has two; **27.** C, Explanation: In both question shapes half the total shapes are shaded, as is the case in C; **28.** A, Explanation: The values represented in the bar charts equal 16, as does the total described in pie chart A; **29.** B, Explanation: Divide the top value of dots by the number below and we get 2 in both question shapes; this is also the case with shape B; **30.** A, Explanation: Neither question shape has any lines of symmetry, nor does J. H has two and O an infinite number.

Find the shape that completes the series

31. A, Explanation: The bar across the circle is rotating in an anticlockwise direction; **32.** C, Explanation: The smaller circle is sinking downwards while the line across the circle is rising; **33.** A, Explanation: The direction of the arrow head is alternating; the number of dots is increasing by 2 each step; **34.** A, Explanation: Each pattern comprises two right-angled triangles and three equilateral triangles forming a random pattern. In each case two of the triangles are shaded. The triangles that are shaded could be two right angled, two equilateral or one of each. In the question shapes we have two shaded equilateral triangles and one of each, so this leaves two shaded right-angled triangles as the next step in the series; **35.** C, Explanation: The shaded segment is rotating anticlockwise around the circle, in turn covering up the shapes in the other segments; **36.** A, Explanation: Both the shaded box and the two shapes are rotating around the shape in a clockwise direction; **37.** B, Explanation: In the series the triangle becomes a square and then turns back to a triangle again; the arrow direction reverses each step; **38.** A, Explanation: The number of triangles increases by 2 each step and the shading of the circles starts on the left and migrates across the shape, one circle each step in the series; **39.** C, Explanation: The number of circles is increasing by one each step and half the total area of the circles is shaded; **40.** A, Explanation: The shapes drop down the square each step, returning to the top of the square each fourth step. They also decrease by one each step, counting down 3, 2, 1, before becoming 3 again, the triangles are all shaded and the whole of the left-hand column is shaded alternative steps; **41.** C, Explanation: The total number of sides of the shapes increases by 3 each step in the series, starting with 9 sides; **42.** A, Explanation: At each step shapes transform; first squares become triangles then arrows become diamonds and finally circles become crosses; **43.** C, Explanation: The number of circles is decreasing, 3, 2, 1 and back to 3 again, and they are moving down the square; the three wavy lines are moving up the square;   **44.** B, Explanation: The L shape rotates around the box in a clockwise direction; at each step a circle becomes a triangle and the shading alternates between the circles and triangles;   **45.** B, Explanation: The number of shaded squares increases by five each step, starting with five shaded squares;   **46.** C, Explanation: A new feature is added to the shape each step and the triangles become squares and then circles before becoming triangles once more;   **47.** C, Explanation: The number of shaded circles and crosses is decreasing by one each step while the direction of the line of circles and the position of the crosses are alternating;   **48.** B, Explanation: Shapes are transformed alternately from circles and squares into semi-circles and triangles. The circles and squares are arranged to the left while the semi-circles and triangles are arranged to the right;   **49.** B, Explanation: The number of triangles that form a random pattern alternate from 7, 14, 7, 14;   **50.** A, Explanation: The total number of sides of the shapes is increasing by 2 each step; the number of sides starts with 4;   **51.** C, Explanation: The number of arrows follows the sequence of square numbers, starting 4, 9, 16, 25 (2×2, 3×3, 4×4, 5×5);   **52.** A, Explanation: The squares decrease in number starting with 4 and alternate from the top to the bottom of the box; the circles increase from one each step and also alternate position;   **53.** B, Explanation: The sequence of segments in the circle follows the BOMAS rule, $6 \div 2 = 3 \times 2 = 6 + 2 = 8$. BOMAS is the order in which operations are undertaken: brackets, of division, multiplication, addition, subtraction;   **54.** A, Explanation: The L shape rotates around the box in an anticlockwise direction; the shapes alternate between squares and triangles arranged left and then right; the wavy lines do not change;   **55.** B, Explanation: The second shape is the mirror image or reflection of the first so the third image in the series must be the mirror image of the fourth which is B;   **56.** A, Explanation: The shading and unshading of the boxes is alternating and the number of shaded or unshaded boxes is increasing by 3 each step, starting with 9. So the series runs 9 shaded, 12 unshaded, 15 shaded, 18 unshaded;   **57.** C, Explanation: The number of sides of the shapes increases by one each step from 9, 10, 11, 12;   **58.** B, Explanation: The number of squares follows the sequence of prime numbers beginning 2, 3, 5, 7;   **59.** B, Explanation: At each step a square is transformed into two triangles and moves down the box; also, there is one less wavy line each step;   **60.** C, Explanation: The inner circle is rotating anticlockwise exposing two shapes each move, the outer circle is rotating clockwise; the shapes are following the sequence square, diamond, circle, triangle and back to square etc again;   **61.** B, Explanation: The numbers on the top line of the shapes count down from 6, 5, 4, 3, the numbers on the bottom of the shapes count from 0, 1, 2, 3;   **62.** B, Explanation: The hands of the clock are indicating the sequence 2, 3, 4, 6 (which are the factors of 12, excluding 1 and 12);   **63.** B, Explanation: At each step the figure is rotating and is the reflection of the previous figure;   **64.** A, Explanation: The number of squares is decreasing by one each step and rotating around the boxes in an anticlockwise direction;   **65.** B, Explanation: The shapes alternate between diamonds and squares and they are rotating clockwise;   **66.** C, Explanation: The shapes start in position C then make a 360° rotation then a 180° rotation then a 90° rotation;   **67.** B, Explanation: Each step in the series the shape is rotated a ¼ turn and then its reflection is represented;

68. A, Explanation: The sequence of shapes runs cross, triangle, circle and square and these shapes are uncovered as the semicircle rotates clockwise;   **69.** C, Explanation: The series of shaded squares are the sum of the multiples of 6, 5, 4, 3 up to 30, ie in the first step of the series the 6th, 12th, 18th and 24th squares are shaded, in the next step the 5th, 10th, 15th, 20th, 25th and 30th squares are shaded;   **70.** C, Explanation: The shape is rotated 90° each step and represented as the reflection of the previous figure; **71.** B, Explanation: The shape is alternating between a hexagon and a square and the number of triangles represents the multiple of 7, 0, 7, 14, 21;   **72.** B, Explanation: The series runs along the top then the bottom of each shape and through the sequence 0–6 starting with 3, so the series runs 3, 4, 5 ,6, 0, 1, 2, 3;   **73.** A, Explanation: The two lines are progressing across the box from left to right; the smaller circle is descending while the line enclosed within the larger circle is ascending;   **74.** B, Explanation: The shaded squares represent the multiples of 7, 8, 9 and 10 up to 30. In suggested answer B the 7th, 14th, 21st and 28th boxes are shaded, the 8th, 16th and 24th in the second step in the sequence and the 9th, 18th and 27th in the next step;   **75.** A, Explanation: In the series the circles have a value of +1, the diamonds –1 and the squares are the product of the sum at that point, so the series runs 4 –2 = 2 + 2 – 3 = 1 + 3 – 2 = the answer, 2 squares;   **76.** B, Explanation: The three shaded squares are moving in a clockwise direction around four adjacent squares;   **77.** C, Explanation: The number of lines and circles is represented; each is represented 1, 2 or 3 times, also either a square, diamond or triangle is represented;   **78.** B, Explanation: Triangles each have a value of +1, shaded squares = –1 and circles give the sum of the calculation at that point. So the series runs 4 – 2 = 2 + 3 – 1 = 4 + or – 0 – 2 gives the answer 2, or two circles;   **79.** B, Explanation: The shaded squares are moving up the grid diagonally from left to right;   **80.** C, Explanation: There are either one, two or three lines on the base of the figure and at the end of the 'arms' either a triangle, square or circle; the arms alternate in direction. The figure with three lines at its base and circles at the ends of the upward-facing arms correctly completes the series.

Completing the series in columns and rows

81. C, Explanation: Each row is made up of the three shapes; the square is missing in the third row;   **82.** B, Explanation: Each column and row comprises the three shapes (only the circles are shaded);   **83.** C, Explanation: Each column and row comprises the three shapes and alternate shapes are shaded;   **84.** A, Explanation: The first two shapes are combined to make the third in each column;   **85.** B, Explanation: A circle with no shading and two types of shading is represented in each row and column;   **86.** A, Explanation: The third shape in each column is the sum of the first shape minus the second. Column 1 has 4 squares – 1 square = 3 squares, column 3 has 1 square – 1 square = no squares;   **87.** C, Explanation: Each row comprises three identical shapes, one with a spot, one with a diagonal line; **88.** C, Explanation: The middle number of lines in each column is divided by the first number of lines to give the third. So 111 ÷ 1 = 111 (3 ÷ 1 = 3), 6 ÷ 3 = 2;   **89.** C, Explanation: The lines attached to the first two shapes in each row are both present in the third shape;   **90.** A, Explanation: Each shape is represented in each column three ways: shaded, large and small; the line across the shapes does not change size;   **91.** C, Explanation: In each row the details within the first two shapes are combined to create the third shape;   **92.** B, Explanation: In each row the number of lines decreases by one;   **93.** B, Explanation: In the columns the shapes combine, except where the feature is repeated in which case it is deleted;   **94.** A, Explanation: The sequence relies on the following values across the rows, taking the first shape in the first column and the first shape in the second column, then the second shape in the first column and the second shape in the second column; a circle + a square = a square, a square + a circle = a square, a circle + a circle = a square, a square + a square = a circle. The answer obtained is square + circle = square, circle + circle = square, giving answer A, square and square;   **95.** C, Explanation: Across the rows each shape rotates to have the other shapes connected to it. Starting on the left the shape at '9 o clock' has the other two shapes connected to it, it then appears at '12 o clock' and then at the '6 o clock' position;   **96.** B, Explanation: In the columns the shapes combine to form new shapes, except where features of the shapes are repeated in which case that feature is deleted;   **97.** C, Explanation: To work out the sequence you need to establish from the two complete rows that a triangle + a square = a triangle, a square + a triangle = a triangle, a square + a square = a square and a triangle + a triangle = a square;   **98.** A, Explanation: Going down each column the L shape is rotating in the first column anticlockwise, the second clockwise and the third clockwise;   **99.** A, Explanation: Going down the columns the shapes combine to form the third shape, except where the feature is repeated in which case it is deleted;   **100.** A, Explanation: Going across the rows, to answer the question you must establish from the two complete rows that $0 + x = x$, $x + 0 = x$, $x + x = 0$, $0 + 0 = 0$.

Mechanical comprehension

101. B, Explanation: The most accurate assessment is most likely to be obtained with the eye directly above both the scale of the measure and the mark on the item being measured;   **102.** A and B, Explanation: The radio produces heat (thermal energy), as a by-product, and sound waves (kinetic energy); it uses electrical energy but does not produce it;   **103.** B, C and D, Explanation: The chemicals in the firework will be transferred into heat, light and sound which are thermal, electromagnetic and kinetic energies;   **104.** Ice, Explanation: The stronger forces give the ice a definite shape;   **105.** A, Explanation: The attractive forces between the molecules forces a liquid into a spherical shape, which has the smallest area for a given volume;   **106.** B, Explanation: The adhesive force between the water and glass is greatest in the narrow tube and the water will rise highest; this is called capillary rise;   **107. and 108.** B and A, Explanation: The meniscus of mercury is convex while the meniscus of water curves downwards;   **109.** B, Explanation: The bar will expand as it is heated so the pins will be pushed away from the blocks;   **110.** Winter, Explanation: In the summer the wires will expand and so slacken; if this was a summer scene then, come the winter, the wires would break as they contracted with the cold;   **111.** A, Explanation: The thicker glass beaker is more likely to crack because the glass on the inside expands while the outside glass does not;   **112.** B, Explanation: When heated, brass expands more than iron so the strip will bend with the brass on the outside as it will become longer than the iron;   **113.** A, Explanation: Water is unusual in that it is most dense at 4°C; most other liquids expand uniformly as they warm;   **114.** B, Explanation: Some water will rise up the tube as the air cools and contracts; this will cause the water level in the beaker to fall;   **115. and 116.** A and F, Explanation: Once the switch is closed the circuit will be complete and the light will come on and the heating element will warm. As the bimetallic strip warms it will bend away from the contact point, breaking the circuit;   **117.** D, Explanation: The behaviour of a gas is described by Boyle's law which states that pressure × volume = constant figure;   **118.** The copper bar, Explanation: Glass is an insulator not a conductor of heat, metals are good conductors and copper is a better conductor than iron;   **119.** B, Explanation: Of the three liquids, mercury has the highest boiling point, alcohol the lowest;   **120.** B, Explanation: A flow of air would occur from the cool sea to the warm land, making the flag fly on the landside of the pole;   **121.** The shiny tin can, Explanation: The shiny can will reflect much of the radiated heat from the sun while the mat black one will absorb most of the heat;   **122.** B, Explanation: In the northern hemisphere the most effective direction for the solar panel would be south facing;   **123.** C, Explanation: The direction of North is given and from this you can work out the other directions;   **124.** C, Explanation: The latent heat of fusion of water is 340,000 joules per kilogram. This is the amount of heat needed to change 1 kg of ice into water without changing the temperature;   **125.** B, Explanation: Mineral salts lower the melting point of water so the temperature of the salty water must be lower than 0°C;   **126.** C, Explanation: The pressure on the ice of the weighted thin wire will melt the ice immediately below the wire. The wire will move downwards but the water above the wire will refreeze. So the block will remain unchanged as the wire slowly passes through;   **127.** C and D, Explanation: Impurities such as salt will cause the boiling point of the water to rise so the water will come off the boil, the temperature of the water will increase and it will come back to the boil;   **128.** B, Explanation: At sea level water boils at 100°C. When the pressure is lower, as it is at altitude, it will boil at a lower temperature;   **129.** B, Explanation: Weight is the force of gravity caused by the pull of the Earth. This effect is slightly greater at the poles so the weight would be slightly heavier;   **130.** B, Explanation: The beams in both A and B can bend; however, in the triangle a bend in one of the lengths would cause tension or compression in another part of the same, making it much more ridged;   **131.** C the least, B the most, Explanation: Both ice and oil float on water so they are less dense;   **132.** Bottom, Explanation: Pressure increases with depth;   **133.** C, Explanation: Pressure acts in all directions but the pressure at the bottom of an object is greater than at the top (this results in an upward force);   **134.** A petrol, B ice, Explanation: Ice is denser than petrol so it will sink below the petrol;   **135.** A, 970 mbar, Explanation: The atmospheric pressure is usually lower when we experience a weather system that brings rain;

136. B, Explanation: Friction acts between two objects when they are in contact and resists movement;   **137.** D, Explanation: Friction can only act where contact exists; all the other forces listed can act at a distance;   **138.** Between 4 and 5, Explanation: The vehicle accelerates quickly between 1 and 2, more slowly between 2 and 3, slows dramatically between 3 and 4 and travels at a constant speed between 4 and 5;   **139.** All three, Explanation: All three are in equilibrium in that they are not moving; C is the least stable as it would take little to change its centre of gravity, A is in neutral equilibrium as its centre of gravity would not change if it was moved;   **140.** B, Explanation: The centre of gravity is the point at which a shape balances; it is the point where it seems as if the whole weight of the object acts;   **141.** C and F, Explanation: The potential chemical energy is transferred into kinetic energy (the moving bullet and sound), heat and light;   **142.** The force, Explanation: The large gear A makes one full turn, the smaller gears two full turns. It will therefore turn more slowly and with a greater force;   **143.** C, Explanation: C shows distance increasing against time, ie accelerating. B shows a constant speed and A is a stationary object;   **144.** Cannot tell, Explanation: Machine 2 brings greater mechanical advantage as the effort required to move a weight is around half that required by machine 1. However, we cannot know where the smaller effort is because we do not know the relative weights of the loads;   **145.** D, Explanation: The direction alternates between the cogs; the cog with 5 teeth is rotating at 60 revolutions per second so the cog with 10 teeth is rotating at 30 revolutions a second;   **146.** C, Explanation: One side is concave, the other convex;   **147.** A and C, Explanation: Like poles repel, opposite poles attract;   **148.** 7, Explanation: They are red, orange, yellow, green, blue, indigo and violet;   **149.** A, Explanation: The incomplete diagram shows 4 A (amperes) going out so 4 A must be supplied;   **150.** B, Explanation: The electrodes and current would cause electrolysis and break the water down to hydrogen and oxygen. The composition of water is H^2O, so for every oxygen molecule there are two hydrogen. There would be therefore twice as much hydrogen produced as oxygen. Experience shows that the hydrogen would be produced at the negative electrode (the cathode);   **151.** Circuit 1 and table 1, circuit 2 and table 2, Explanation: The light comes in circuit 1 only when A and B are both closed. In circuit 2 the light comes on when either switch A or B is closed;   **152.** At no point, Explanation: Gamma rays are highly energized and, while reduced by a thin sheet of lead, are not completely stopped;   **153.** B, Explanation: Betaparticles are fast-moving negative electrons that pass through cloth, paper etc but are stopped by dense substances such as aluminium;   **154.** A, Explanation: Alpha particles are positively charged and relatively large and slow. They are stopped by most materials, including paper;   **155.** C, Explanation: A hydroelectric energy source relies on water turning a turbine which is then converted into electric energy by a dynamo;   **156.** Both A and B, Explanation: The downward acceleration of the balls would be the same; the horizontal acceleration of ball B does not affect this so they would hit the ground at the same moment;   **157.** Cannot tell, Explanation: If the tyres were inflated to the same pressure then you could tell that B carried the greatest load but without this information you cannot tell;   **158.** All equal,

Explanation: The pressure is consistent throughout the fluid;   **159.** A, Explanation: The weight × distance in A is equal on both sides, all the others are unequal, so the seesaw would move.

IQ tests

160. C, Explanation: A spells humbug, B hullabaloo;   **161.** D, Explanation: The sequence is the multiples of 8, 8 × 2 = 16, 8 × 3 = 24, 8 × 4 = 32 and so on;   **162.** E, Explanation: This is the name for one of the continents; all the others are types of fabric;   **163.** C, Explanation: Divide the middle number of each set by the first number to get the sum on the right;   **164.** C, Explanation: Starting with 7 and going anticlockwise add 1, then 2, then 3, then 4, eg 10 + 3 = 13 + 4 = 17;   **165.** B, Explanation: A spells quarter, C spells quarrel;   **166.** C, Explanation: This is a type of stool; the others are types of chair;   **167.** C, Explanation: The sequence is the multiples of 6 starting with 11 × 6 = 66;   **168.** E, Explanation: Multiply the previous sum by 2 and deduct successively 2, 3, 4, 5 etc. Eg 24 × 2 = 48 − 3 = 45, 45 × 2 = 90 − 4 = 86;   **169.** Primitive;   **170.** A, Explanation: This is the only country in the list that does not include a letter 'u' in its English spelling;   **171.** D, Explanation: The sequence is taken from the multiples of 9 starting with 6 × 9 = 54;   **172.** C, Explanation: in rows 6 − 4 = 2, 8 − 6 = 2, 14 − 10 = 4, in columns 6 + 8 = 14, 4 + 6 = 10, 2 + 2 = 4;   **173.** A, Explanation: B spells fathom and C fault;   **174.** B, Explanation: Baleen is a type of whale; all the others are types of bridge;   **175.** D, Explanation: The numbers in the right-hand set are 2 less than their corresponding numbers in the left-hand set;   **176.** D, Explanation: Divide the middle number by the number on the left to get the right-hand number, eg 36 ÷ 6 = 6;   **177.** E, Explanation: The sequence is taken from the multiples of 7 beginning with 7 × 8 = 56;   **178.** pp, Explanation: Platypus, an egg-laying Australian mammal;   **179.** B, Explanation: This is a peninsula in northern Europe; the rest are geological periods;   **180.** C, Explanation: A spells matter, B grumpy and D greasy;   **181.** C, Explanation: Divide the middle number by the number on the left: 49 ÷ 7 = 7;   **182.** D, Explanation: Going clockwise add 3, then 4, then 5, then 6, eg 1 + 3 = 4 + 4 = 8;   **183.** AAA, Explanation: The word is Rastafarian, a religion that follows the teachings of Haile Selassie;   **184.** C, Explanation: Divide the middle number by the one on the left, eg 45 ÷ 9 = 5;   **185.** B, Explanation: Going anticlockwise, double the sum and deduct successively −1, −2, −3, −4, −5, eg 20 × 2 = 40 − 3 = 37;   **186.** A, Explanation: This is a type of fuel; the rest are types of energy;   **187.** B, Explanation: The numbers in the right-hand set are six higher than the corresponding number in the left-hand set;   **188.** duplicate;   **189.** D, Explanation: This is a group of musicians; the others are types of music;   **190.** EEE, Explanation: Engineer;   **191.** D, Explanation: Going anticlockwise starting with the question mark the series is formed from the multiples of 12 beginning 3 × 12 = 36;   **192.** C, Explanation: This is the surname of a famous physicist; the rest are names of types of star;   **193.** A, Explanation: B spells define, C decide and D deduce and educed;   **194.** C, Explanation: They are the first five whole cubed numbers (1×1×1, 2×2×2, 3×3×3 etc);   **195.** D, Explanation: This is an example of a name; all the others are types of name;   **196.** hydrangea;   **197.** E, Explanation: This is a relative of the rhinoceros; the rest are types of knot;   **198.** D, Explanation: Add the first two numbers in each set and then divide the sum by 2 to get the third number. Eg $3 + 3 = 6 \div 2 = 3$;   **199.** bb, Explanation: rhubarb;   **200.** E, Explanation: This is a large rodent from South America; all the others are types of monkey;   **201.** B, Explanation: The sum of the numbers in the same position of each set is 10;   **202.** E, Explanation: This is the first name of a painter, Pablo Picasso; the rest are types of painting;   **203.** C, Explanation: The letters spell 'lunacy';   **204.** D, Explanation: The sum of each set of numbers is 16, $2 + 6 + 8 = 16$;   **205.** outrageous;   **206.** A, Explanation: Granite is a type of rock, the others are types of mineral (rocks are made of minerals);   **207.** A, Explanation: It is the series of the first 5 even numbers; the answer could have been 10 but this was not one of the suggested answers; note that all even numbers end in either 0, 2, 4, 6 or 8;   **208.** A, Explanation: This is a type of singer; the rest are types of instrument;   **209.** B, Explanation: Circle A spells satire, C spoof, D lampoon (B spells parade);   **210.** A, Explanation: The number in the second group is one more than its corresponding number in the second group;   **211.** E, Explanation: All the others are types of alloy while silver is a pure metal;   **212.** moccasin;   **213.** B, Explanation: The series is formed from the first 6 squared numbers (1×1, 2×2, 3×3 etc);   **214.** F, Explanation: All the others are cities that have hosted the Olympic Games;   **215.** oo, Explanation: Cormorant;   **216.** B, Explanation: the others are types of story;   **217.** C, Explanation: Subtract successively 6, 5, 4, 3, 2 , $15 - 5 = 10$;   **218.** D, Explanation: This is a story or myth; all the rest are types of novel;   **219.** D, Explanation: A spells mother, B father, C guardian (D spells grandson);   **220.** A, Explanation: This is a type of flat; the rest are types of house;   **221.** C, Explanation: The sum of the numbers in the corresponding positions of both groups is 6;   **222.** rrr, Explanation: Gerrymander;   **223.** D, Explanation: This is a type of boot; the rest are types of shoe;   **224.** E, Explanation: The numbers count 0–8 starting with the first number in the first set, then the first number in the second set and so on;   **225.** C, Explanation: This is a shape while all the others are names of types of triangle;   **226.** latitude;   **227.** C, Explanation: It is a type of seabird; all the others are types of fish;   **228.** B, Explanation: The numbers are all factors of 18 (divide exactly into 18);   **229.** A, Explanation: The letters spell minutiae, B spells dislike, C intend, indent and tinned and D assemble;   **230.** E, Explanation: A marrow is a vegetable; the others are types of cereal;   **231.** D, Explanation: Going clockwise, subtract the second number from the first to get the next number in the series;   **232.** B, Explanation: This is a type of pea; all the others are types of bean;   **233.** rhombus, Explanation: A rhombus is a diamond-shaped figure;   **234.** C, Explanation: This is a flat surface; all the others are types of shape.